WHY ME?

WHY ME?

A. J. Matthews

VICTORY PRESS

EASTBOURNE

ISBN 0 85476 176 4

Printed in Great Britain for
VICTORY PRESS (Evangelical Publishers Ltd)
Lottbridge Drove, Eastbourne, Sussex
by Richard Clay (The Chaucer Press) Ltd,
Bungay, Suffolk

Contents

FOREWORD

To explain and justify to men the ways of God is a task inseparable from the Christian ministry. Few aspects of pastoral work entail such soul-searching, or require such agonising honesty as this.

It is so easy to be facile! Cliches by the score are at hand to help us out of the corners we so often find ourselves in. But they do not satisfy—either those we seek to comfort, or, least of all, ourselves.

Where can we find real help? I believe there are two unfailing sources of instruction: the teaching of God's Word and the experience of God's people.

In the course of a pastoral ministry extending over 30 years, and an itinerant evangelistic ministry covering a further 10 years, it has been my privilege to meet many splendid servants of God, albeit some of them in very humble walks of life, who have taught me lessons which I have so absorbed that they have become part and parcel of my being, and for which I shall be eternally grateful. Much of what follows is a distillation of the things I have learned from them. It represents the gleanings of the years.

But basic to everything is the plain teaching of Scripture. It just cannot be ignored. The philosopher attempts to unravel the mysteries of life, but with

few exceptions God is left out of account in the process. To ignore God, however, is surely to ignore
the *one great abiding reality*. No attempts at ex-
plaining human suffering, or solving the problems
it presents to men's minds, can hope to succeed
on such a basis. And because we believe God has
revealed himself within that book we call the Bible
the light it sheds is indispensable. In this connection I owe a considerable debt to the writings
(unfortunately long out of print) of the late Dr. A.
T. Pierson. It seems to me that he, more than most,
penetrated to the heart of the matter. Certainly I
can say that as I have put what I have received to
the test, throughout the years I have felt firm ground
beneath my feet, and have been able to impart solid
consolation in many a time of need.

If by this book I can help someone else to understand, I shall be more than satisfied.

A. J. MATTHEWS

PART ONE

Grappling with the Problem

CHAPTER ONE

The Problem of Suffering

THE PROBLEM OF SUFFERING is a bigger problem for a Christian than for an atheist. It seems to me that the atheist, completely uninfluenced by Christian thought, cannot enter into it. In its most intense form it is occasioned by the Christian doctrine of the love of God and the difficulty of squaring that with the sad and bitter facts of life as people experience them daily.

Looking at mankind in the mass, we see millions of human beings under-nourished through famine, under-privileged, homeless and destitute as a result of war, enslaved and hopeless—the victims of world-shaking events over which they had no control.

Turning from the mass to the individual, the picture comes into sharper focus. A mother struggles year in year out to support her children while her husband's mistress lives in idle luxury.

A child is born with fingers protruding from his shoulders where his arms should be—the result of the carelessness of society, and the unwitting actions of his parents, as in the case of the thalidomide babies.

An alcoholic is driven to suicide by the demons his corroded mind conjures up. Siamese twins are born—all their life long they will suffer the degradation of being stared at whenever they appear in public.

It is pointless to go on. The tragic story of human suffering has no end.

The problem is compounded further by the fact that in so many instances the suffering seems to fall on decent, innocent people, while the scoundrels seem to get away with things scot free!

Centuries ago the psalmist was distressed by this. He saw the wicked spreading himself like a green bay tree; he was envious at his prosperity. He noticed that the wicked 'were not in trouble as other men'. All too often the swindler, the cheat and the oppressor seemed able to escape unscathed. The contrasts of life are unbelievable. Some persons are virtually untouched by personal suffering. It seems as if some golden hand guides their affairs from the cradle to the grave. In other instances every breath drawn is pain and anguish, and every moment seems an eternity for the suffering it contains.

Most puzzling of all, however, is the seeming indifference of God to what is going on. In face of all the suffering, and the inequitable state of affairs, to many people God appears silent and unconcerned. It would seem He neither knows nor cares. The words of Job find an echo in the hearts of sufferers everywhere: 'Let me know why Thou dost contend against me.'[1] They echo loudest from the hearts of Christians.

No Simple Answer

One thing needs to be noted at this point: we need not expect to find any simple answer to the problem.

To say the Bible has a clear cut answer to every problem is foolish. It has not. We are called upon to walk by faith, not by sight. A great deal remains to be revealed which we cannot bear now. The sufferings of mankind are infinitely complex and the explanations must be complex also. To quote Paul: 'Now we see in a mirror dimly, but then face to face. Now I know in part; then I shall understand fully, even as I have been fully understood.'[2]

Does this mean that there is no point in searching for an answer? Not at all. Our affirmation is that within the Bible answers are given which cannot be found elsewhere. If they do not afford enough light to solve *every* problem at least they provide enough light to live by—and in any case they far outshine the philosophies of men.

Atheism, with its doctrine of contingency, can explain things only in terms of luck.

Fatalism, with its doctrine of necessity, offers no comfort to a mind distressed.

The natural religions of the world have nothing to offer comparable to the Christian revelation.

We turn to the Bible believing that our cry for light in the darkness will not go unheeded altogether. That light might be only a glimmer, but it will grow brighter as it shines more and more unto the perfect day.

CHAPTER TWO

The Bundle of Life

WE ARE 'bound in the bundle of life.'[1] So said Abigail to David as she pleaded for the life of her husband and kinsfolk. She expressed a profound truth. Human society is organised in such a way that each member affects and is affected by the actions of every other member. We form a 'body'. 'If one member suffers,' says Paul, 'all suffer together.'[2] Words spoken of the church, but equally true in a general sense.

Since we are part and parcel of human society, neither you nor I can escape this involvement. We have a direct connection with the whole human race. We are members one of another. A large part of human suffering finds its explanation in this fact.

A septic wound in the finger can distribute its poison through the whole body till the person is sick from head to foot. By the same token, a strong and healthy heart can communicate its vitality with equally far-reaching effects. So it is with the body of humanity. There is no escaping from one another —for good or ill.

Unfortunately the society with which we are associated is basically a sick society. The race of which we form a part is a fallen race, subject to mortality and all the ills that precede it. Human suffering began with the first catastrophic act of rebellion when man pitted his will against the will of his Maker, and chose his own way in life; and suffering has continued ever since. You and I are involved because of our connection with those who have gone before. From our first parents we have received a nature tainted with sin and a body destined to death and dissolution. All human suffering is traceable, ultimately, to this fact.

Heredity has to be reckoned with in relation to man's spiritual being, as in relation to his physical nature, if we are ever to understand why men suffer. 'Man is *born* to trouble as the sparks fly upwards.'[3]

But this law of mutual involvement, based on the organic unity of the race, operates not only in respect of the remote past, it operates today.

A mother and her children, living in some small town, suffer untold humiliation and shame, not for anything they have done, but because their father is a murderer. Had any other man been the father things might have been different. They suffer purely on account of their association with him. A child is hopelessly crippled and condemned to a spinal carriage for the rest of his life because someone else carelessly dropped him as an infant. A child is born with the seeds within him of mental and physical disease destined to develop in later years, simply because his parents were who they were. '... visiting the iniquity of the fathers upon the children to the third and fourth generation.'[4] Whether we like the idea or not, the words ring true to life. This is the way it is.

IS THIS ARRANGEMENT JUST?

The questions that now arise are these: Is this arrangement just? Can it be reconciled with belief in a God of infinite justice and love? Why should children suffer for their parents' sins or because of the carelessness of other people? Could not some better arrangement have been made? Such questions are inevitable and they demand an answer. Fortunately it is to hand. Consider for a moment: There is a bright side to this arrangement as well as the dark side we have just presented.

A man works hard and by his skill, personality and integrity, raises himself to a position of wealth and of honour in public affairs. His wife is honoured with him. She sits beside him on important platforms and society people court her company. His children benefit also. They are in the public eye. They attend the finest schools and have the very best education. They have a great many advantages other people's children lack. Neither this man's wife nor his family have done anything personally to deserve these benefits. They possess them solely because of their connection with a man who has made good in life. He is honoured and all his family is honoured with him.

At the time of writing, the daily newspapers reported the story of a young man and woman who were adopted years before, in early childhood, by a man who was then relatively poor. In the course of years this man succeeded in business and acquired great wealth. Now, upon his death, the two adopted children find themselves heirs to money running into millions of pounds sterling!

Here we have this same law of life working itself out, not for ill but for *good*. How strange that no one complains of injustice in such circumstances as these. We may envy the young folk their good fortune, but we do not complain about it. Yet if someone suffers because another person has embezzled a sum of money, they are apt to complain bitterly about the injustices of life and to blame God for the way the world is run. The truth is that people want to eat their cake and have it too. It is impossible to have a law operating in one direction only. This law of organic unity upon which human life is based was designed by the Creator for man's benefit. When it operates to man's hurt it is because man has perverted that law by his own stupidity or plain cussedness. The fault is man's not God's. We need to recall the finish of that ancient saying:

God visits 'the iniquity of the fathers upon the children to the third and fourth generation of those who hate me, but showing steadfast love to *thousands* of those who love me and keep my commandments'.[5]

SOME CONCLUSIONS

From the consideration of these facts a flood of light falls upon a number of relevant issues. In the first place we have here an adequate explanation of a great deal of the suffering in the world. When, for instance, we are involved in sickness, bereavement or financial loss due to the failure of others, we should not be surprised. Human nature being what it is, and human society being organised in the way it is, these things are inevitable. Man remains a fallen, fallible and mortal creature, heir to everything that goes with these characteristics. We cannot justly blame God for these happenings.

Once this law of the unity of the race is really grasped, we shall have no difficulty in understanding why the innocent suffer with the guilty. To many people this is a tremendous problem. But the answer is simple; the innocent suffer with the guilty for the same reason that the undeserving prosper with the prosperous: *because the life of each affects the lives of all*. It is impossible to have a law operating for man's advantage that cannot be turned to his disadvantage if he so chooses. The innocent suffer because of man's irresponsibility in frustrating God's intentions in the way He has ordered our lives. It is as simple as that.

This unity of the race is the fundamental principle upon which our redemption in Jesus Christ is based. We have seen how an undeserving person can be benefited through association with someone else who has made good in life, as easily as the opposite can happen. When we lift this principle out of the realm of ordinary affairs up to the level of spiritual and eternal affairs what amazing grace we see. You and I, who deserve nothing of God but His displeasure and wrath, are accepted by Him in love and favour, not for anything that we have done, but because of what another has done; not for any merit on our part, but solely because of the merit of Jesus Christ our Lord. If by living faith we join ourselves to Him, then, because we are His, we are *accepted in*

Him. The victories He won He shares with us; the inheritance He gained is our inheritance too. There is nothing unusual in all this. It is in perfect keeping with the way God works in every realm of human life. If it be true that when one member suffers all the members suffer with it—by the same token it is possible for the One member to be honoured and all the members to be honoured with Him.

This unity of the race provides hope for the future. As we receive a heritage of woe, so we can *start* a heritage of blessing. The misery may extend to the third and fourth generation, but the blessing can flow on through thousands of generations. A man can enter this life under the burden of a background which is vicious and evil, and by the grace of God he can get rid of that burden and pass on to his children a heritage of good far exceeding the other both in scope and permanence. Hence we see our responsibility towards other people. No man can live to himself alone, no matter how he tries. Willy-nilly, everything he does affects others for good or ill. I may cause the innocent to suffer, or I may miss the chance of being made a blessing. My way of life is not just my own affair, something to be decided wholly and solely by my own desires. I am my brothers' keeper.

> We do not pass this way alone;
> This we know full well;
> Either we lift men up to heaven,
> Or we drag them down to hell.

We are bound up together in the bundle of life.

CHAPTER THREE

Reaping the Whirlwind

'YOU ASKED for it, and you've certainly got it!' The remark is a familiar one. It reminds us that a great deal of the suffering we endure we bring on ourselves. We call the process retribution. Retribution is the act or process of re-tributing, or paying back, It is clearly recognised in the Bible as a fact of life.

The rule of justice in the Old Testament was 'life for life, eye for eye, tooth for tooth'. We are told that every transgression received a 'just retribution'.[1] Adam and Eve were punished for their disobedience by being excluded from the tree of life. Cain, for the murder of his brother Abel, was banished from society. Haman, plotting the death of Mordecai, was hanged on the gallows he himself had prepared. Judas destroyed himself by the betrayal of Jesus.

Communities are not exempt: Sodom and Gomorrah were burned to the ground because of the depravity of the inhabitants and the disease this depravity brought with it. Israel was taken into captivity because of the nation's forgetfulness of God. Jerusalem was sacked by the Romans in fulfilment of Christ's prediction that this would be her fate for her rejection of Him.

If we turn to modern times, examples are furnished by the long series of trials of Nazi war criminals. For many years the despots of Auschwitz, Dachau and other Nazi extermination camps lived unpunished, but eventually their crimes caught up with them and they met with retribution. The classic case of Eichmann, one of the worst of them all, provides an example known throughout the world.

In each of these instances, the suffering entailed was retributive—the evil done was paid back to the offender. He was given his deserts.

Is This Right?

How are we to regard suffering of this kind? Paul writes to the Thessalonians and says: God 'deems it just to repay with affliction those who afflict you'.[2]

The writer to the Hebrews says: 'If the message declared by angels was valid and every transgression or disobedience received a just retribution how shall we escape if we neglect such a great salvation?'[3]

Paul writes to the Romans and speaks of 'the day of wrath when God's righteous judgment will be revealed. For He will render to every man according to his works'.[4]

The radical philosopher objects to all this. He deems the idea of retribution unenlightened, savage and un-Christian. We need to be clear on this issue. Does retribution have an abiding place in the economy of God? Can it be justified? I believe it does, and it can.

In essence retribution is the protest of eternal righteousness against sin. It is a protest which must be made. God cannot approve of wilful sin, or even be indifferent to it, without losing His own perfection and ceasing to be worthy of our worship and adoration. His very being compels Him to disapprove, and to be real that disapproval must be impressively expressed. The only just and proper way in which it can be expressed is in the form of suffering meted out to the offender. Suffering of this kind is part of the system by which God exercises His moral government in the world. It forms a part of the 'wrath of God', which Bishop Handley Moule defines as 'the sinless aversion of holiness to sin'. The penalties which are attached to untruth, impurity and unrighteousness, for instance, are to be seen as the 'outflashings of that holy anger which is founded in God's love of the right, the true, the pure'.

Without such a protest the divine disapproval could be overlooked and moral standards abandoned altogether. These can still be abandoned, of course, despite the protest, such is the blindness of men to their own best interests, but at least when disaster strikes God is exonerated. We have been warned. Those who ignore the red light do so on their own responsibility.

SIN IS SELF-RETRIBUTIVE

Retributive suffering is not arbitrary. It is important that we grasp this. Many forms of wrong-doing hold within themselves the seed of their own punishment; in other words they are self-retributive.

I have in my files, notes of the case of a man I visited several times in a Glasgow hospital. He was in a ward for mental patients because, although he was completely lucid at some times, at others he became violent, losing himself in a screaming frenzy. He was nearly 60 years of age. The Jewish consultant in charge of him, told me that the fits were due to toxins having affected his brain as the result of venereal disease of very long standing. Thirty or forty years earlier this man apparently had had an illicit sexual union, and now, after all those years, his sin had caught up with him. My friend did not know the connection between his present trouble and the lapse of so many years before, and the doctor did not propose to tell him, but the connection was there. This was a clear case of retribution. The Bible does not say 'Be sure your sin will be found out', it says 'Be sure your sin will find you out'.[5]

This is a much deeper and more significant truth. 'Whatever a man sows, that he will also reap. For he who sows to his own flesh will from the flesh reap corruption.'[6] This is a statement of one of the most basic and unalterable laws of human life—as the drug addict and the alcoholic eventually discover, along with many others who abuse God's gifts and flout His laws.

I recall the saying: If a man breaks the laws of nature, nature has a way of boxing his ears. We sow to the wind and we reap a whirlwind.

A Christian recognises that the laws of nature are simply what man has discovered of the will and ways of God, and in this particular feature of life he sees the sovereignty of God at work building retribution into its very fabric, not as an arbitrary judgment, but as the inevitable concomitant of wrong-doing. Says Denny, 'Punishment is as inseparable from sin as heat is from fire.'

RETRIBUTION HERE AND HEREAFTER

The Bible makes it plain that retribution operates both here and hereafter.

In this present world it is expressed in physical and mental suffering and in calamities of various kinds; in the hereafter it is to be expressed in eternal judgment and perdition.

Sometimes people say, 'I believe a man makes his own hell here and now.' So he may; but we make a great mistake if we limit retribution to this life, and if we think that death brings it to an end. Far too much unrewarded goodness and unrequited wrong exists in the world for there not to be a day of reckoning in the afterlife.

'It is appointed for men to die once, and after that comes judgment.'[7] Death is not the end. There is the afterwards which has to be faced. There are books which have to be opened and read. There is justice to be done.

RETRIBUTION IS OFTEN INCOMPLETE

Thus far our consideration of this subject has been comparatively plain sailing, but now we come to the problem which lies at the heart of the matter. So often retribution in this life seems to be incomplete or avoided altogether. It raises a big question as to why it should be so. If everyone who formed an illicit sexual union suffered as our friend suffered whose case has just been cited, there would be at least some show of equality about the ways of God, but everyone knows that this does not happen. It appears that in some instances men are able to sin with impunity and heaven is indifferent to what is going on. Each successive generation has been conscious of the anomaly. Is there an answer to it? Possibly not in the sense that something can be said that removes the problem completely, but perhaps we can relieve it in part.

SIN IS INCOMPLETE

Sin is often incomplete and therefore retribution may well be incomplete. The judgment of God upon the Amorites was held up for centuries because, as was said, their iniquity was 'not yet complete'.[8] Their wrong-doing had to take its full course and work itself out to fruition before it could be adequately and justly judged. This principle applies not only to nations, but to individuals as well. Until he reaches the end of life a man's sin is incomplete and it is therefore fitting that the judgment of God upon that sin should be incomplete. Indeed, the very nature of retribution is that it is the final chapter of the story—the grand denouement.

BUT GOD IS GRACIOUS

There are considerations of a happier sort, and among them this, that God waits to be gracious. Judgment, we are told, is His 'strange work'. He 'delighteth in mercy'.

Written deep in the heart of the Old Testament, so often misrepresented in its teaching concerning the character of God, is the statement that God takes no pleasure in the death of the sinner, but rather that he shall turn from his wickedness and live.

He is a God 'Merciful and gracious, slow to anger, and abounding in steadfast love and faithfulness.'[9] The supreme proof of this is the Cross of our Lord Jesus Christ, for by that unique event a method of mercy was opened up, contrived in the heart of the eternal God, whereby men may receive the divine forgiveness and be saved from the penalty of their wrong-doing.

This method of mercy does not operate by *averting* the proper retribution due to sin, but by *diverting* it to the head of the sinner's substitute. Isaiah declares, predicting the sufferings of Jesus: 'He was wounded for our transgressions, He was bruised for our iniquities; upon Him was the chastisement that made us whole . . . and the Lord has laid on Him the iniquity of us all.'[10]

Peter speaks of Christ: Who 'Himself bore our sins in His body on the tree'.[11] At the Cross eternal righteousness made its protest against human sin. Retribution fell in fullest measure.

In those dreadful moments of desolation, when He cried 'My God, My God, why hast thou forsaken me?' Jesus tasted the horror of damnation. In this divine protest the principles of eternal justice can be seen to be upheld. The just deserts of human sin were meted out. They were accepted and borne by the One who stood in the sinner's place. They were absorbed by Him in the immensity of His grief and anguish until they were exhausted and there was

nothing left of the wrath of God to be endured—
nothing left but endless blessing to be received by
all who believe in Him.

> O Christ, what burdens bowed Thy head!
> Our load was laid on Thee.
> Thou stoodest in the sinner's stead,
> Dids't bear all ill for me.
> A victim led, Thy blood was shed;
> Now there's no load for me.

Personal retribution, therefore, may well be sus-
pended until God sees what men will do with the
mercy and forgiveness offered them in Christ Jesus.
The sinner may yet repent and turn from the evil of
his ways: so justice stays her hand.

THE TEMPORAL AND THE ETERNAL PENALTY

Sometimes forgiveness and a measure of retribution go together. In other words, while the spiritual
and the eternal consequences of sin may be can-
celled, the temporal penalty may be allowed to remain. David provides us with a classic example of
this in that his child, born of his adulterous union
with Bathsheba, was taken from him by death, although David's sin had been forgiven. The words of
the prophet Nathan are very significant: 'The Lord
also has put away your sin; you shall not die. Nevertheless, because by this deed you have utterly scorned
the Lord, the child that is born to you shall die.'[12]
Matters were put right between David and God, but
the temporal punishment had still to be endured as a

discipline, and also as a visible protest against the wrong done. God frequently acts in this way. Many a person has found that while grace gives a man a new nature, it does not necessarily give him a new body, and that the physical marks and scars of sin have a way of remaining long after the sin has been forgiven.

IT IS AVOIDABLE

From all that has gone before, it is obvious that retribution is a form of suffering that is avoidable. The psalmist says: 'Many are the pangs of the wicked; but steadfast love surrounds him who trusts in the Lord.'[13]

There are forms of suffering which may well be inevitable, but retribution is not one of them. No man need suffer this unless he makes it certain by the way of life he chooses. If we learn the simple lesson that the pathway of obedience to God is the pathway of our highest happiness and our greatest good, and that disobedience always brings unhappiness and misery, and if we carry out that lesson in practise, we shall spare ourselves a great deal of needless sorrow.

DO NOT JUDGE OTHERS

One note of warning is to be sounded. We must resist the tendency for this aspect of suffering to exclude from our minds virtually every other consideration. To the Jews of the Old Testament times, retribution was the whole answer—goodness is rewarded, wrong-doing is punished. Much prosperity predicates great goodness and much affliction predicates great wickedness. To them it was as simple as that. To some people it tends to be this way still.

A young woman, living in south-west London, one of the pluckiest persons I have ever known, was a great sufferer. She was also a person of tremendous Christian faith, who accepted her suffering as from a heavenly Father's hand. Imagine her feelings when an earnest Christian friend, referring to her complaint, exclaimed one day: 'There must be some great sin in your life for you to suffer so.' It was a remark of unbelievable cruelty; alas, the story is true.

We need to remember constantly, especially in our judgment of others, that while suffering *may* be retributive it is equally possible that it may not be so. We shall see later that it may well be a token not of God's anger *but of His love.* In any particular case, we are not to judge lest we ourselves be judged.

How to Take It

If we are conscious that we are suffering for our own wrong-doing, what should be our attitude? How should we take it?

One thing is sure; it is futile to react with resentment and rebellion. The only thing to do is to accept the discipline, humbly and penitently, recognising its justice, and the wisdom and love of God which lie behind it.

Two bandits were crucified with Jesus. They suffered retribution for their misdeeds. One reacted with violent taunts as he vented his spleen on the innocent victim on the central cross. 'Are you not the Christ?' he railed, 'Save yourself and us!'[14]

The other bandit rebuked him: 'Do you not fear

God, since you are under the same sentence of con-
demnation? And we indeed justly; for we are re-
ceiving the due reward of our deeds; but this man has
done nothing wrong.' And he said, 'Jesus, remember
me when you come in your kingly power.'

And Jesus said to him, 'Truly, I say to you, today
you will be with me in Paradise.'

This second man did not beg to have his punishment removed, or be delivered from the agony of
the cross. He agreed with the sentence. He appeared
truly penitent; for one sure mark of genuine repen-
tance is that the offender, even though it be at cost
to himself, is content to suffer so that the law and
character of God should be vindicated. He is prepared to take his medicine without complaint.

This positive approach to suffering which we
might have brought upon ourselves, is not only the
right one, it is the best one; for accepted in this way
the suffering becomes productive of much good. The
negative approach accomplishes nothing except to
sink us deeper into our embitterment and despair.
For men of humility and faith, even retribution can
cease to be a curse and can be transmuted into a
blessing.

CHAPTER FOUR

Perfect Through Suffering

'IT HURTS ME more than it hurts you!' How often have we who are parents said this to our wriggling offspring in the course of administering a spanking! The child finds it hard to believe—yet is it not true?

The infliction of pain is not always an expression of vengeance, it *can* be an expression of the most intense love and concern.

The writer to the Hebrews says: 'The Lord disciplines him whom He loves, and chastises every son whom He receives. It is for discipline that you have to endure. God is treating you as sons; for what son is there whom his father does not discipline?'[1] And he goes on to say that if his readers are without any discipline, then it is obvious that they are not in the family—they simply don't belong. A father disciplines members of his own family; he does not discipline other people's children.

God can allow suffering to overtake you and me, in love, because He designs the suffering to teach us lessons we need to learn in order to correct our faults and failings.

In our characters there may be chaff that needs to be sifted from the wheat, dross that needs to be separated from the gold, roughnesses that need to be removed, sharp corners that need to be rounded off. Suffering can be a sieve, a furnace, an abrasive, a file with which God does His work. He can take the suffering resulting from our own sin and folly, as well as that resulting from the actions of others, over which we have no control, and direct it to our benefit.

The prophet Jeremiah complained about the pride of Moab in these terms: 'All his life long, Moab has lain undisturbed like wine settled on its lees, not emptied from vessel to vessel; he has not gone into exile, (banished from his homeland). Therefore the taste of him is unaltered, and the flavour stays unchanged.'[2]

There is nothing to equal being emptied from vessel to vessel, being poured out of one situation into another, for changing the flavour of a man's life. Better than anything else, this can shatter our self-sufficiency, humble our pride and correct our faults.

There is much we can learn from the story of Peter's shameful denial of Jesus. Jesus told him that before the cock crew Peter would deny Him three times. But having said this, Jesus did not indicate any desire that Peter might be spared this experience. All He said was, 'Peter ... I have prayed for you that your faith may not fail.'[3]

Sometimes break-down and failure in our lives, and all the consequent suffering, are allowed, and God makes no effort to stop them, because He knows that only through such bitter experiences shall we learn the truth about ourselves and find the way to better things. Before his denial of Jesus it was all 'I' with

Peter. 'Lord, I am ready to go with You to prison and to death ...'[4] 'Though they all fall away because of You, I will never fall away ... Even if I must die with You, I will not deny You.'[5]

Poor Peter! So sure of himself. So ignorant of the weakness of his own nature. So reluctant to take precautions and pray. So insulted by the idea that he of all people should ever deny his loved Master and Friend. What a lot he had to learn! Jesus knew that there was only one way he could learn it—and it just had to be the hard way. So the Master's prayer for Peter was not that he should stand firm amidst temptation, but simply that through the shame and disgrace of failure, his faith might not fail. He was not altogether to be kept from falling, but Jesus desired that he might be kept from falling altogether. And this prayer was heard.

Peter denied his Lord, as predicted, but he emerged from the experience a changed man. Chastened, humbled, broken-hearted, penitent, a sadder but wiser man, he was recommissioned by the risen Christ, as an under-shepherd of the flock of God, and privileged to preach the sermon which, on the day of Pentecost, produced 3,000 converts to the faith. What a comeback!

BURNING IN THE BEAUTY

Suffering, however, is permitted to enter our lives not only to correct our faults, but also to develop our virtues.

During a visit to a West of England pottery one day, I learned something more about our subject. I watched the whole process of making pots, from start to finish. I saw the clay being taken out of the sodden clay pit; I saw it broken down in water and emptied from vessel to vessel, the impurities being gradually discarded in the process; I saw it on the potter's wheel, and stood entranced at the shapely forms which grew under his skilful hand; after that the pots were decorated with colourful designs, then dipped in a substance which hid the colour and left them all a greyish white. Then they were fired.

During the final process of firing I was invited to peer through a peep-hole into the kiln. I shall never forget the dramatic sight I saw. The inside of the kiln was filled with hundreds of pots piled skilfully, one on top of the other. As the flames played upon them and the heat increased, the greyish-white glaze became transparent, and presently the whole kiln was filled with colour, as the hidden decorations came to light.

I learned that day that God does not put us into the furnace necessarily to burn up the dross that may be in us, sometimes He puts us there to *burn in* the beauty.

As there are vices which only suffering can cure, so there are virtues which only suffering can produce. Forbearance can be cultivated only under provocation; patience only under constant trial; faith only when the way is dark; obedience only under test; self control only under crisis; sympathy only as we pass the bitter way ourselves; humility only under failure; submission only in face of the cross.

There is no other way.

Turning to the letter to the Hebrews we read: God 'disciplines us for our good, *that we may share His holiness* ... later it yields the peaceful fruit of righteousness to those who have been trained by it.'[6] Paul writes to the Romans: 'We rejoice in our sufferings, knowing that suffering produces endurance, and endurance produces character, and character produces hope, and hope does not disappoint.'[7]

James writes: 'Count it all joy, my brethren, when you meet various trials, for you know that the testing of your faith produces steadfastness.'[8]

It is not by chance that some of the world's greatest saints have been the greatest sufferers. Some flowers yield their sweetness only to the night air. I remember reading of an old master in the art of making violins who always used wood from the north side of the tree for his instruments. He found that the wood which had stood the brunt of the cold fierce wind, icy snow and raging storms, gave a finer tone to the violin and produced sweeter music.

Of the many fine people I have been privileged to meet in my life, two who impressed me more than most were a humble Scottish local preacher and his wife. He was terribly crippled and in poor health, but his wife was the greater sufferer. When I knew her she had been in bed 14 years with her limbs completely locked by arthritis. She lay with her head on the pillow and the bed-spread tucked under her chin. All I ever saw of her was her face. The only movement she was able to make was a slight turning of her head upon the pillow from right to left. I never even saw her hands. Yet to enter that home was a benediction. Never once did I hear her complain. All the talk was of the goodness and love of God, and of His perfect wisdom in all His ways. One left the home humbled and awed by such faith. Many a time I recalled the lines:

'Heroes are forged on anvils hot with pain,
And splendid courage comes but with the test.
Some natures ripen, and some natures bloom
Only on blood-wet soil; some souls grow great
Only in moments dark with death or doom.'

A tremendous fire swept over 150 miles of the Pyrenees. It burned up vineyards, oliveyards and dwellings, but it was the means of revealing rocks and exposing great veins of precious metal.

Many a fire sweeping over the lives of God's people has revealed unsuspected qualities of rock-like faith and patient endurance, which have been greatly to the enrichment of those concerned, and to the glory of the One they serve.

Suffering has often been God's instrument in leading men back to Himself.

'Far too well your Saviour loves you
To allow your life to be
One long calm, unbroken sunbeam,
One unruffled, stormless sea;
He would have you fondly nestling
Closer to His gentle breast;
He would have that world seem brighter
Where alone is perfect rest.'
                                    Author unknown

A young man lay in hospital stricken with polio. An early faith had died away, and for several years he had cared nothing for the things of God. Now, in his extremity, he called upon God again and promised that if God would restore him he would devote the rest of his life to God's service. Today he holds an honoured place in the Christian ministry. During World War Two, a woman of my acquaintance told the following story of her life. She and her family were at home when a bomb fell, destroying their house and killing her husband. With her daughter, she moved to a new home and began to gather up the threads of life again. Then another bomb fell, destroying her second home and killing her only child. Disconsolately she moved into a third house. Once again a bomb destroyed it, and this time she herself was buried beneath the rubble, escaping with her life as by a miracle. Then she thought to herself: 'God must surely have a plan and a purpose for my life to have spared me like this. If so, I want to know what it is.' Before long she had sought and found the Lord.

So it is that in the discipline of suffering Christian faith can be produced and perfected. I know only too well that suffering does not always produce faith —that sometimes it produces atheism. Why this should be is the subject of a later chapter. All I am saying at the moment is that suffering *can* bring men to God, and that this can be a valid explanation of why it is allowed.

PREPARATION FOR SERVICE

Suffering is a powerful factor in preparing us for fruitful service.

In Paul's letter to the Corinthians we find some illuminating words—he speaks of the 'God of all comfort, who comforts us in all our affliction, so that we may be able to comfort those who are in any affliction, with the comfort with which we ourselves are comforted by God'.[9] I never read these words without recalling the instance of a business man from the Lancashire town of Preston. Late in life a daughter was born to him, an only child, who grew to the age of six or seven. One day she fell against a glass cabinet, breaking the glass. She did not appear to be badly cut, but before long she became very ill, and it was found that her brain had become infected. Ultimately she died, without the doctors being able to account for the course of events. How the infection had reached her brain was a mystery. As the child lay in her coffin her broken-hearted father stooped to kiss her brow. As he did so, his lip was pricked by something sharp. Her shrinking skin had bared a tiny sliver of glass which had entered above her eye, and had led to her death. The good man was a Christian and faith survived the devastating blow.

A short while after this incident, our friend took a business trip to America. On board ship his attention was drawn to a fellow passenger who seemed morose and withdrawn. Cultivating his company, our friend from Preston found that his companion had once been a believer in Christ, but had lost his faith and was bitter and resentful. To the amazement of our friend, he discovered that his companion had recently lost his daughter in circumstances which almost exactly matched his own. She, too, had fallen against a glass cabinet and had died as a result. There in mid-Atlantic the two men talked it over. Gradually the bitterness subsided, the resentment melted away, faith returned, and before the voyage was over a shattered spirit was restored to faith and hope.

Now it is true to say that no one in the whole world could have ministered to that stricken spirit but the one who had passed that precise way himself. We comfort others with the comfort wherewith we ourselves have been comforted of God.

Alexander Whyte, the famous preacher of Free St. George's Church, Edinburgh, was an illegitimate child. Throughout his life he laboured under this sorrow; but who can tell how much that powerful ministry owed to the burden that lay so heavily upon him?

They say no musician reaches the heights of musical expression until his heart has been broken. Bread corn has to be bruised.

If God is going to use us to feed the hungering souls of men, we should not be surprised if we have to go through the mill first.

Our Great Pioneer

It was this way with our Master.

In the Letter to the Hebrews it is written: 'It was fitting that He, for whom and by whom all things exist, in bringing many sons to glory, should make the pioneer of their salvation perfect through suffering."[10]

Even our Lord Christ was not exempt. He had to become Himself a man of sorrows and acquainted with grief, before He could be the Saviour of the world. If, then, it was necessary for Him, how much more it is for us. Only by experience can we truly enter into the sufferings of others, and be of help.

CHAPTER FIVE

Flung Down in the Mud

JOB'S SUFFERING is proverbial. But I wonder if we realise just how intense it was, and how important the Book of Job is to an understanding of our subject from a Christian angle. It presents the problem of suffering in classic terms.

The stage is set as the world's greatest saint is presented as the world's greatest sufferer; and the question is asked, Why? Greatest saint! Greatest sufferer! To grasp the measure of the problem we need to sense the meaning of 'greatest' in each connection, and to this end we must at least know the substance of the story.

'There was a man in the land of Uz, whose name was Job; and that man was blameless and upright, one who feared God, and turned away from evil.'[1] So the book opens.

Later we find that God speaks, repeating the commendation, not once, but twice, and adding, as He addresses Satan, these significant words: 'He (Job) still holds fast his integrity, although you moved me against him, to destroy him *without cause.*'[2]

Blameless! Upright! God-fearing! One who turns his back on evil! Loyal in his faith! And all to a degree beyond that attained by any other person!

This is God's estimate of Job. As we read on in the story the details are filled in.

In his family relationships Job was an example. We read that when his sons had finished their feasting Job 'would send and sanctify them, and he would rise early in the morning and offer burnt offerings according to the number of them all: for Job said, "It may be that my sons have sinned, and cursed God in their hearts." Thus Job did continually'.[3]

It is fascinating indeed to read chapter 29 and see the kind of life Job lived and the circumstances surrounding him before calamity overtook him. Here are a few illuminating phrases:

'In the days of old,' he says, 'God watched over me . . .'

'His lamp shone upon my head . . .'

'My children were about me . . .'

'My steps were washed with milk . . .' (indicating his affluence)

'The rock poured out for me streams of oil . . .' (oil was wealth in those days as today)

Job goes on to describe the respect paid to him by his fellow citizens:

'When I went out to the gate of the city, when I prepared my seat in the square, the young men saw me and withdrew, the aged rose and stood . . .'

'Princes refrained from talking, and laid their hand on their mouth . . .'

'The voice of the nobles was hushed, and their tongue cleaved to the roof of their mouth . . .'

Next he describes his generosity :

'I delivered the poor who cried . . .'
'I caused the widow's heart to sing for joy . . .'
'I put on righteousness, and it clothed me . . .'
'My justice was like a robe and a turban . . .'
'I was eyes to the blind . . .'
'I was feet to the lame . . .'
'I was father to the poor . . .'
'I searched out the cause of him whom I did not know . . .' (The poor man's lawyer)
'I broke the fangs of the unrighteous, and made him drop his prey from his teeth . . .'
'Men listened to me, and waited, and kept silence for my counsel . . .'
'I chose their way, and sat as chief, and I dwelt like a king among his troops, like one who comforts mourners.'

What a man Job must have been—an Eastern Sheik of unchallenged authority, an oil king of immense wealth, but using his advantages for the benefit of his fellows. The greatest of all the men of the East.

JOB'S SUFFERING

Now this greatest of men is allowed to undergo the greatest suffering. Blow after blow falls upon him. It begins as his oxen, asses, sheep and camels are all either killed by lightning or captured by the Sabeans—eleven thousand five hundred animals in all. A bitter blow indeed—but things could be worse: he still has his servants. Then word comes that his servants have been killed by the Chaldeans.[4] This is a further blow—but he still has his family to comfort him. Then he hears that his seven sons and three daughters are all dead.

A servant brings the news: 'Your sons and daughters were eating and drinking wine in their eldest brother's house; and behold, a great wind came across the wilderness, and struck the four corners of the house, and it fell upon the young people, and they are dead.'[5]

This is the bitterest blow of all—but he still has something to be thankful for; he has health and strength. But not for long.

The day comes when he is afflicted with loathsome sores from the crown of his head to the soles of his feet.[6] So unbearable is the irritation that he takes a potsherd and scrapes himself among the ashes.

He describes his condition:

'My bowels are in a ferment and know no peace . . .'
'Days of misery stretch out before me . . .'
'My blackened skin peels off . . .'
'My body is scorched by the heat . . .'[7]
'By night pain pierces my very bones . . .'
'There is ceaseless throbbing in my veins . . .'
'My garments are all bespattered with my phlegm which chokes me like the collar of a shirt.'[8]

Things are bad with Job indeed: possessions gone!
Servants gone! Children gone! Now health gone!
Only one thing in life is left to support him; he still
has his wife. This means a lot. No man is completely
desolate, even in the direst affliction, who has a loyal
and devoted wife to support him. And Job still has
his wife. Or has he?

The day comes when his wife turns on him and
says, 'Do you still hold fast your integrity? Curse
God and die!'[9]

Now public disgrace follows private calamity. His
closest friends who come to comfort him rub salt
in his wounds by accusing him of hidden sin. They
pulverise him with words and insult him with self-
righteous accusations. The youths of the city, who
before had paid him deference, now make sport of
him. They stone him as he walks the streets. They
flaunt their violence in his face, no longer fearing
his power.

No wonder Job cries: 'God Himself has flung me
down in the mud, no better than dust or ashes.'[10]

In agony he appeals for understanding: 'Have pity
on me, have pity on me, O you my friends, for the
hand of God has touched me.'[11] Did anyone suffer as
Job suffered? Could anyone deserve it less?

The world's greatest saint is the world's greatest
sufferer!

Why?

In circumstances like these it is inevitable that the
sufferer asks: Why? And Job was human like the
rest of us. Inevitable also that there should be plenty

of people anxious to offer an answer. So Job's friends gather round him, and present their solutions to his problem. Eliphaz, Bildad and Zophar take turns to speak.

His friends maintain that Job's suffering is retributive. It is punishment for some hidden sin. They call on Job to come clean and confess the wrong he has done.

'What innocent man has ever perished?' they say.
'Where have you seen the upright destroyed?'[12]

When Job protests his innocence, they speak of

'the long-winded ramblings of an old man . . .'[13]
'this spate of words . . .'
'nonsense . . .'
'God exacts from you less than your sin deserves . . .'[14]

So they insinuate Job's guilt.

When Job refuses to agree with them they grow more and more candid in their opinions:

'Do not think that He reproves you because you are pious, that on this count He brings you to trial. No: it is because you are a very wicked man, and your depravity passes all bounds . . .'[15]
'Come to terms with God and you will prosper; that is the way to mend your fortune . . . He will deliver the innocent, and you will be delivered, because your hands are clean.'[16]

The answer they give is the traditional one, reflecting the ancient philosophy of suffering, that all earthly calamity is a punishment of sin, and earthly success a reward of virtue. They have no other answer. Is it any wonder that Job is infuriated? No wonder he calls his friends, 'Miserable comforters!' Miserable comforters indeed. They just do not have a clue.

GETTING NEARER TO IT

The next to take the stage is Elihu. He is a young man, and he is angry. While Eliphaz, Bildad and Zophar were talking he had been an impatient listener. He became more and more exasperated as Job appeared to make himself more righteous than God, and as Job's friends completely failed to justify God's ways. Now he gives his answer. In substance it is that Job is wrong to ask: Why? Addressing Job, Elihu says: 'You have said your say, and I heard you. "I am innocent," you said, "and free from offence, blameless and without guilt. Yet God finds occasions to put me in the wrong and counts me His enemy; He puts my feet in the stocks and keeps a close watch on all I do." Well, this is my answer: *You are wrong.* God is greater than man; why then plead your case with Him? for no one can answer His arguments.'[17]

'Far be it from God to do evil or the Almighty to play false . . .'

'The truth is, God does no wrong, the Almighty does not pervert justice . . .'[18]

Elihu continues: 'The Almighty we cannot find; his power is beyond our ken, and His righteousness not slow to do justice. Therefore mortal men pay

Him reverence, and all who are wise look to Him.'[19]

Elihu's philosophy is that of reverent agnosticism. God is so great, we are so small; God is so infinite, we are so finite; we cannot hope to know His reasons for what He does. The best we can do is maintain our faith in His justice, and, in spite of all, bow humbly before His almighty power. At one or two points in his speech, Elihu has a dim glimpse of the disciplinary aspect of suffering, but he continually falls back on the idea that the meaning of suffering is too great a mystery for mortal man to solve. 'God's power is beyond our ken.'

Now there is a great deal to be said for any philosophy which humbles man before his Maker. Pride is one of the seven deadly sins, and to be made to feel the greatness and grandeur of God, and our own limitations, is good for all of us. Although Elihu is the youngest of Job's friends, he gets closest to the heart of things, and this God recognises.

Now God Speaks

In some of the grandest prose in the English language, God's words are presented to us as He continues Elihu's theme, cutting Job down to size, and contrasting man's puny powers with the marvellous power of God displayed in nature.

Job is impressed.

'What reply can I give thee, I who carry no weight? I put my finger to my lips. I have spoken once and now will not answer again; twice have I spoken, and I will do so no more.'[20]

'I have spoken of great things which I have not understood, things too wonderful for me to know. I knew of Thee then only by report, but now I see Thee with my own eyes. Therefore I melt away; I repent in dust and ashes.'[21]

Job has no more to say. But still his question remains unanswered: Why me?

THE REAL ANSWER

The book of Job belongs to the Wisdom literature of the Hebrews. A characteristic of these writings is that while a clear problem is posed the answer is hidden; it has to be deduced, or sought for in some other way. Ecclesiastes is constructed in this way; so is Job.

To find the real reason for Job's sufferings, therefore, we have to go back to the opening scenes in the drama. There we see Satan sneering at Job's piety and questioning his motives. Satan suggests that Job's godliness is really nothing more than enlightened self-interest. Job serves God simply for the material and temporal blessings he enjoys by God's favour.

Satan says to God: 'Has not Job good reason to be God-fearing? Have you not hedged him round on every side with your protection, him and his family and all his possessions? Whatever he does you have blessed, and his herds have increased beyond measure. But stretch out your hand and touch all that he has, and *then he will curse you to your face*.'[22]

So the Lord gives Satan permission, and the first round of disasters falls upon Job.

But Job does not curse God. He holds fast to his faith and his integrity is unshaken.

So Satan tries again. 'Skin for skin,' he says, 'There is nothing the man will grudge to save himself. But stretch out Your hand and touch his bone and his flesh, and see if he will not curse You to Your face.'[23]

So the Lord gives Satan permission, and the final disasters overtake Job. But through it all Job does not utter one sinful word.

'If we accept good from God,' he says, 'shall we not accept evil?'[24]

So Satan's attack is defeated and the sincerity of Job's faith is demonstrated.

But whom was Satan really attacking? On the face of it he appeared to be attacking Job, but in reality, behind his attack on Job there was an oblique attack on God, who was his real target. If Satan could have demonstrated that God was incapable of holding a man's loyalty and trust apart from the material blessings God gave him, Satan would have destroyed God's character. If Job had failed under the test how Satan would have taunted God!

'Look,' he would have said, 'Job did not love *you*, he loved only the things you gave him. You had to bribe him to hold his devotion. He didn't serve you for what you are—in fact he didn't serve you at all, he merely used you to serve his own interests. The moment you deprived him of his possessions he threw you over, showed his true colours and made it plain that he despised you. So, you see, you are not the wonderful person you are made out to be. See—he is cursing you to your face!'

But Job did not fail under the test. He refused to curse God. Out of the depths of his misery he cried:

'He knows the way that I take; when He has tried me I shall come forth as gold.'[25]

Magnificent!

In all this Job won a double victory; he vindicated his own sincerity of faith, and the character of God. He demonstrated that to him God was a wonderful person, capable of holding Job's esteem and reverence, even though He allowed Job to be deprived of every earthly good, and rained on him blow after blow.

Now the importance of what Job did, and what noble sufferers who have echoed his words since, have done, cannot be over-estimated. By and large Christians are fairly prosperous in relation to this world's goods. The virtues Christianity tends to produce are those which make for success in life, 'Godliness is of value in every way,' we are told, 'as it holds promise for the present life and also for the life to come.'[26] But is this the reason why we love and serve God, and worship Him?

The cynic says it is.

'Faith,' he says, 'is just enlightened self-interest.'

'Christianity is no more than veiled materialism.'

'People are godly for gain.'

'Religion, you must admit, is not without certain business advantages.'

If these charges could be universally sustained it would indeed be the death of God and an end of Christianity. Christians would be seen to be no longer worshipping the Creator, but only the gifts He gives them: the homes, gardens, fine clothes, television sets, cars and gadgets we prize so highly. God would become an inglorious being surrounded by sycophants pursuing His favours, and ready to desert Him the moment those favours are withdrawn.

It is imperative, therefore, that in every generation there should be some who demonstrate the genuineness of Christian faith and the sincerity of their worship by maintaining these even in the face of total calamity.

Seen in this light many a life which appears to be useless becomes a life of inestimable value to the kingdom of God, and the advancement of the faith. Here is a man, for instance, stricken with a permanent disability. Unable to maintain his family as he has been accustomed to, he suffers the constant humiliation of having to depend on charity for his livelihood, and on other people for his mobility. What can redeem his self-respect, justify his continued existence or make life worthwhile? On the face of things he appears a useless encumbrance to himself and other people. Not for this person is the thrill of so-called Christian service, or of public acclaim. He cannot preach, or teach a class, or serve on a committee, or even head a subscription list. He can do none of these things which we imagine earns us a star in our crown.

But is this really so? Or can he? I believe this man

may one day find a star in his crown of the most brilliant order. In maintaining his faith in the face of adversity he *demonstrates the glory of God.* Such an example confounds the devil, shuts the mouths of the cynics, imparts dignity to the sufferer, encourages others to hold on, and makes life worth living. The world just cannot afford to be without such persons.

Suffering may be allowed in our lives to discipline us, but it may also be allowed because God has such confidence in the sincerity of our faith that He knows we will not let Him down. To be allowed to suffer in this way is to have paid to us the highest compliment that Deity can pay to man—it is *God's vote of confidence in us.*

Job asked : Why me ? At last he has his answer !

CHAPTER SIX

For Others

ONE ASPECT OF SUFFERING clearly is distinct from anything we have considered so far: I refer to vicarious suffering.

The word vicar denotes a person who has been deputed to perform the functions of another. A substitute, in other words. Vicarious suffering, therefore, is suffering voluntarily entered into in the place of, or on behalf of, another. It is a type of suffering which reaches a plane infinitely higher than any other. No type of suffering is more noble than this.

Now we know that a great deal of suffering is unavoidable; it comes to us, for one reason or another, in the permissive will of God, and we can do nothing but accept it, joyfully or otherwise. But vicarious suffering is something we deliberately expose ourselves to. It is very much a part of human life.

A physician investigates a rare disease, in consequence he contracts the disease and dies. A stewardess returns to a crashed and burning plane, to rescue some injured person who cannot help himself, and in so doing sustains serious burns and is scarred for life.

A widow half starves herself to scrape enough money together to send her son to college.

A father impoverishes himself paying the debts of

a worthless son, in order to save his son from prison
and the family from disgrace.

All these are examples of vicarious suffering. In
each instance the individual concerned deliberately
chose to expose himself by becoming involved with
the problems of others. Without suffering of this kind
how much poorer the world would be!

HE DIED FOR ALL

It is not surprising that we find vicarious suffering
at the very heart of the Christian gospel, for the
supreme example of it is found in the sacrifice of
Jesus Christ our Lord. 'Greater love has no man than
this, that a man lay down his life for his friends.'[1]

One's life is one's most precious possession. When
we *choose* to lay down *our lives* for others we offer
the greatest demonstration of love anyone can make.
Jesus *chose* the road to Calvary. And He chose *to die*.

He said explicitly: 'No one takes (my life) from
me, but I lay it down of my own accord. I have power
to lay it down, and I have power to take it again.'[2]

Again, to Pontius Pilate, the Governor, at the time
of His trial, Jesus said: 'You would have no power
over me unless it had been given you from above.'[3]

Our Lord, therefore, declared himself to be majesti-
cally free in life and death. What took place on Calvary was a voluntary act of self-immolation in order
to secure the redemption of the world. Even when
His soul recoiled in horror at the prospect of His
sufferings He refused to turn back from the path He
had chosen. 'Nevertheless, Father,' He said, 'not my

will but thine be done.'

GOD WAS IN CHRIST

Vicarious suffering is in heart of God. 'God was in Christ reconciling the world to Himself.' 'For God so loved the world that He gave His only begotten Son. . . .'[5]

So read the immortal statement.

The glory of the Christian gospel lies in this: Faced with man's ruin through sin, God Himself chose to become personally involved in man's rescue, even though that rescue meant sacrifice of such infinite proportions as these finite minds of ours cannot even begin to comprehend. As a result, the eternal God, the creator of all things, knows what suffering is, not merely with the knowledge of an onlooker, but with the knowledge of a participant.

Within the sweet society of the Godhead, the relation of perfect love that had ever existed between the Father and the Son, was ruptured, as the Son of God, incarnate as the Son of man, took man's place, bore upon Himself the guilt of the whole human race, and on that account exposed Himself to the righteous judgment of God.

'My God, My God,' He cried, 'why hast Thou forsaken Me?'[6]

That was damnation, it has been said—and He took it lovingly.

None of the ransomed ever knew
How deep were the waters crossed,
Nor how dark was the night the Lord passed through
E'er He found His sheep that was lost.

But that suffering was not His alone. We make a vast mistake if we conceive of the anguish of the Cross as being something exclusive to the Son who hung there. That anguish was equally great in the heart of the Father.

He (God) 'did not spare His own Son', we are told, 'but gave Him up for us all.'[7]

'In this is love, not that we loved God but that He loved us and sent His Son to be the expiation for our sins.'[8]

'God loved the world *so much*. . . .'[9]

To know the breadth and length and height and depth of this love is to understand the heart of God.

As . . . So

The example of our Saviour presents a lasting challenge to us His followers.

On that notable occasion when the risen Lord Jesus appeared to His disciples in the upper room, after they had shut themselves in for fear of the Jews, we are told, He showed unto them His hands and His side. Then He said to them: 'As the Father has sent me, even so I send you.'[10] Both the gesture and the words were intensely significant. From then on the disciples knew the way they were to go and the price they would have to pay. As . . . so . . .

No doubt they would recall the words of their Master on an earlier occasion when He said: 'If any man would come after me, let him deny himself and take up his cross daily and follow me.'[11] People in those days were familiar with the sight of condemned criminals carrying their crosses to the place of execution, but always those prisoners were the unwilling victims of their own misdeeds: their suffering was retributive. With Jesus it was different. He 'took up' His cross, voluntarily, deliberately, as of choice, not to atone for His own misdeeds, but for the misdeeds of others. It was He who said to His disciples: 'As . . . so . . .' From now on the qualification for a man to be one of His followers is a similar willingness to accept whatever measure of suffering may be involved in implementing this work of redemption—even if it means a personal crucifixion. Paul wrote to the Colossians and said: 'It is now my happiness to suffer for you. This is my way of helping to complete, in my poor human flesh, the full tale of Christ's afflictions still to be endured, for the sake of His body which is the Church.'[12]

Wonderful words.

Someone has said: 'Christianity without sacrifice is the laughing-stock of hell.' It is also a contradiction in terms. Vicarious suffering forms a vital part of our Christian calling. Peter writes in his first letter and says: 'Christ also suffered for you, leaving you an example that you should follow in His steps.'[13]

The trouble with so much present day Christianity is that Christians are not prepared to follow *in His steps*. They want to follow, but they do not want to follow the way of the Cross. They seek an easier road. They do not want to get involved. It might hurt. But there is no other way.

'Whoever does not bear his own cross and come after me, cannot be my disciple.'[14] So said our Lord, and He has never taken back His words.

A Rich Reward

One more thing, however, needs to be said: The way of the cross leads to the crown. There are compensations for the hardness we endure. There is an ample reward ahead.

Paul writes to the Romans and says: 'We are heirs of God and fellow heirs with Christ, provided we suffer with Him *in order that we may also be glorified with Him*.'[15]

We read about Jesus, who 'for the joy that was set before Him endured the Cross, despising the shame'.

We are not dealing here with suffering which is the result of wrong-doing on our part, or that which stems from our mortality, or that which comes to us to discipline our lives or test our faith, but that which is deliberately entered into, 'with Christ', that His purposes of worldwide redemption might be achieved. To those who thus, 'complete' His sufferings comes a share in His glory.

SUMMARY OF PART ONE

My suffering may be:	In my case—	
	TRUE	FALSE
1. Due to my mortality and the ills that accompany it. See Chapter One.		
2. Due to my involvement with others in the bundle of life. See Chapter Two.		
3. Due to my own folly or wrong-doing. See Chapter Three.		
4. Permitted as a loving discipline to shape my character and mould my life as God would have it be. See Chapter Four.		
5. God's way of preparing me for more effective service. See Chapter Four.		

6. God's vote of confidence in me, knowing that by my steadfast faith under the test of undeserved suffering, the sincerity of my faith will be demonstrated and God will be glorified.
See Chapter Five.

7. The price I have to pay for my discipleship as I seek to follow the Master in the way of the Cross.
See Chapter Six.

PART TWO

Guidance in the Trial

CHAPTER ONE

God in the Darkness

WHEN GOD wants us to get to know Him better He is apt to hide Himself in darkness. This is one of the strange paradoxes of life.

In the Bible story of the migration of the Children of Israel from Egypt to the Land of Promise, there comes a point at which Moses is to receive the Ten Commandments at the hand of God. It is an awesome occasion.

The tribes have reached Mount Sinai, in the heart of the Arabian desert. As they wait at the foot of the mountain, the earth quakes, the whole mountain trembles, thunder and lightning adds to the terror. Sinai is wrapped in smoke, and a thick cloud obscures it as God descends to meet His people.

Then, as we read the story, we come to these significant words :

'And the people stood afar off, while Moses drew near *unto the thick darkness where God was.*'[1] God in the darkness! Think of that.

Sooner or later in life all of us have our moments of darkness and intense terror—times when the foundations of our life are broken up, when our whole world rocks and tumbles to pieces. At such times it is good to remind ourselves that the darkness

does not necessarily mean that God has forsaken us.
It may very well mean that He is seeking to give us a
clearer revelation of Himself than we have ever had.

Rightly understood, every dark experience in life
is a golden opportunity to get to know God better.

Says the psalmist: 'The Lord is near to the broken-
hearted, and saves the crushed in spirit.'[2]

While the sun shines brightly and our sky is blue,
and all is well with our affairs, it is easy for us to
forget God altogether. We tend to grow self-sufficient,
self-confident, proud. We become more and more
absorbed in our own endeavours, and in consequence
God becomes less and less relevant. But when a halt
is called in our activities, and we are suddenly
plunged into darkness of mind and soul, when deep
sorrow overwhelms us, the situation is radically
changed. Then God has His opportunity. Hiding
Himself in the clouds of our sorrow He invites
us to draw near, enter the darkness and find Him
there.

THE DARKNESS OF SORROW

Bereavement, the sickness of those we love, sudden
and unexpected misfortune, the uncertainty of a livelihood, the ravages of war— these, surely must be
among the most common sorrows of mankind,
casting millions of our fellow men and women into
unutterable darkness of soul. Can we confidently
affirm that in such experiences God is in the darkness? Surely we can.

From time to time there have appeared in history
what might be called representative men; men whose

lives have epitomised the great characteristic experiences of mankind.

One such was Job. All the varied sufferings to which we are heir were combined and concentrated in this one life. War, bereavement, financial disaster, sickness, loneliness, misunderstanding by those nearest and dearest, misrepresentation—Job experienced them all: and experienced them altogether at the same time.

If ever a man knew the meaning of darkness of soul and spirit, Job was that one. Yet what do we find? Job, who at first cried out 'Oh, that I knew where I might find Him!' at the end of his trials was able to say to God: 'I have heard of thee with the hearing of the ear, but now mine eye seeth thee.'

How did Job come to this knowledge? Through his sorrow he had found God in the darkness.

A middle-aged woman, whom I remember well, gave this testimony: 'It was only after I lost my sight and became completely blind, that through my blindness I sought and found God.'

Such instances as these give great encouragement. They help us to believe that, strange and inexplicable as our sorrows often seem to be, there is nevertheless a purpose in them. There amidst the darkness of our human trouble God waits to reveal himself to us more perfectly. Others have proved this true. So may you.

THE DARKNESS OF DOUBT

For the mind to get into a state of doubt and uncertainty, in which nothing is sure, is a very terrible thing to happen. Here is a form of soul darkness which can be truly Egyptian in its intensity. And yet, even through doubt you and I can come to a firmer grip, and clearer knowledge of God than ever before.

That great preacher of a former age, C. H. Spurgeon, at one period of his life, fell into this state of mind. He describes his experience thus: 'The thought came to me that there was no God, no Christ, no heaven, no hell; that all my prayers were but a farce and that I might as well have whistled to the winds or spoken to the howling waves . . . I no longer moored myself hard by the coasts of revelation; I said to reason: "Be thou my Captain"; I said to my brain, "Be thou my rudder" . . . I went to the very verge of the dreary realms of unbelief. I went to the very bottom of the sea of infidelity. I began to doubt if there was a world. I doubted everything, until at last the devil defeated himself by making me doubt my own existence. I thought I was an idea floating in the nothingness of vacuity; then, startled with the thought and feeling that I was substantial flesh and blood after all, I saw God was, and Christ was, and heaven was, and hell was, and that all these things were absolute truths. The very extravagance of the doubt proved its absurdity. When I arose faith took the helm; from that moment I doubted not. Faith steered me back; I cast my anchor on Calvary, I lifted my eye to God: and here I am alive and out of hell. Now, whenever I hear the sceptic's stale attacks upon the Word of God, I smile within myself

GOD IN THE DARKNESS

and think: "Why, you simpleton! how can you urge
such trifling objections?" I have felt in the conten-
tions of my own unbelief, ten times greater difficul-
ties! We who have contended with horses are not
wearied by the footmen.'

Doubting Thomas, of whom we read in the
Gospels, provides another illustration. His soul was
in thick darkness as he said, 'Unless I see in His hands
the print of the nails, and place my finger in the mark
of the nails, and place my hand in His side, I will not
believe.'[3] And yet there came a moment when amidst
the darkness the light broke and he saw the living
Christ, and made such a confession of Him as none
of the other disciples made. 'My Lord and my God,' he
said.

Do not fear the darkness of doubt; draw near in
honesty of heart and sincerity of purpose and you
will find God—even there. John Angell James, celebrated minister of Carr's Lane, Birmingham, said: 'It
is not the mind that never doubted, perhaps because
it never examined or reflected, but that has doubted,
and yet triumphed over its doubts, that exhibits the
strength of true belief.' There are things we know;
there are things we do not know and cannot until
the hereafter. It is folly to let the things we do *not*
know rob us of the light and comfort of the things we
do know. Enough, amidst the darkness, if we know
Him and can say with Paul, 'I know whom I have
believed, and am persuaded that He is able to keep
that which I have committed unto Him against that
day.'[4]

THE DARKNESS OF TEMPTATION

A young fellow, some years ago, walked the streets of Manchester in hell. He was a Christian, but for a week or more his mind had been filled with such a succession of unclean, lascivious, evil, blasphemous thoughts as to be beyond repetition. All his peace was destroyed, and it scarcely seemed possible to him that he could be a Christian at all. Nothing brought relief.

He tried to quote Scripture; he tried to sing; he tried to pray; he tried to distract his thoughts in endless ways, but all to no purpose. At last in utter desperation he sought the advice of an older and more experienced Christian. His friend listened and then referred him to a passage in Bunyan's Pilgrim's Progress for an explanation of his trouble. Now Pilgrim's Progress has not the authority of Holy Scripture, but for all that, Bunyan understood the human heart as few have understood it, and he certainly knew the meaning of temptation. So this young man read the prescribed passage. It had to do with the time when Christian was passing through the darkness of the Valley of the Shadow.

This is what he read :

'One thing I took notice of, that now poor Christian was so confounded that he did not know his own voice; and thus I perceived it.

'Just when he was come over against the mouth of the burning pit, one of the wicked ones got behind him, and stepped up softly to him, and whisperingly suggested many grievous blasphemies to him, *which he verily thought proceeded from his own mind.*

This put poor Christian more to it than anything that he had met before, even to think that he should now blaspheme Him that he loved so much before; yet could he have helped it, he would not have done it; but he had not the discretion neither to stop his ears, *nor to know from whence those blasphemies came.*'

No words could have described more exactly this young man's predicament. For the first time he realised that as the human mind is open to the influence of the Holy Spirit of God, so it is open to the spirit of evil. The vile thoughts that were troubling him were not necessarily his own. As Satan tempted our Lord in the wilderness, putting suggestions to Him that were contrary to God's will, so he can do with us. With this understanding came an immense relief from personal guilt, and also an awareness of the way of deliverance. Instead of using panic methods to try to overcome the problem, the whole matter was laid before God in prayer, with the request that He would deliver from the power of the evil one—that enemy of our peace already vanquished at Calvary. The simple testimony of this young man is that prayer was heard. God was found, and His power to deliver proved, even in the darkness of a temptation as hellish as this. And during a long life the problem has never recurred.

We have to remember that temptation is not sin; it becomes sin only when it is yielded to. Our Lord was sorely tempted, yet He did not sin. Even in the darkness of that final struggle in the garden of Gethsemane when His whole soul was in such agony that

He sweat, as it were, great drops of blood, angels came and ministered to Him. God was there. Even the awful darkness and dereliction of the Cross passed, and the dreadful cry: 'My God, my God, why hast Thou forsaken me?' gave place to His final prayer—quiet and confident—'Father, into Thy hands I commit my spirit.'[5]

So our temptations come, and go. They cast us into darkness, but God is in the darkness holding out to us His strong right hand. We have but to grasp it in faith and commit all to Him, to be brought through triumphantly.

THE DARKNESS OF CONVICTION

'If God Almighty doesn't damn my soul He ought to.' So said a man to me as he strode up and down my study one day.

I shall never forget him. My first contact with him was at a street corner question hour which I was conducting. Standing on the edge of the crowd he called out a question: 'Mr. Speaker, do you believe in reincarnation?' For a moment I was tempted to answer facetiously, but something restrained me and I replied, 'No, I do not. I believe that when our loved ones are taken from us there is no return. David said of his dead child: "I shall go to him, but he shall not return to me." ' And I continued in that strain.

Two days later, in my study, he told me his story. He had been married and for the last 23 years he had been unfaithful to his wife. Six months previous to our meeting she had died. Now he saw what a cad he had been.

'Sir,' he said to me, 'one night she came to me in my dreams and said: "If only you had kissed me before I died;" Another night she came and said, "If only you had been with me when I died!" Sir, is there any chance of getting my wife back to re-pay her for the ill I've done?' (He was in a state of intense tension, pacing my floor like a man demented.)

Of course, I had to tell him that it was too late. He could not undo the past, all he could do was amend the future and live for the rest of his days as his wife would have wished, asking God's forgiveness for the wrong he had done. That was the beginning of a relationship that led ultimately to his conversion, and the acceptance of Jesus Christ as his Saviour and Lord. He put away the woman with whom he had been consorting, brought his aged mother from Edinburgh to keep house for him and altogether mended his ways. His soul had been in the darkness of conviction—but he found God there.

David knew all about this. He, too, had fallen foul of a beautiful woman. Engineering the death of Uriah, he had taken Bathsheba, Uriah's wife, in an adulterous union. Murder and adultery lay at his door.

Listen as he describes his state of mind:

When I declared not my sin, my body wasted away through my groaning all day long. For day and night Thy hand was heavy upon me; my strength was dried up as by the heat of summer.'[6] Loss of weight, mental distress, sleepless nights, physical and nervous exhaustion—the pattern is a familiar one. To be under conviction of sin is no joke. Our mental institutions hold thousands of people who have broken under the strain. They have found the darkness unbearable. Now the prophet Nathan comes to David. Speaking with the authority of God he points the accusing finger and says: 'Thou art the man!' And David repents his sin.

Listen again to what he says: 'I acknowledged my sin to thee, and I did not hide my iniquity; I said, "I will confess my transgressions to the Lord"; then thou didst forgive the guilt of my sin.'[7] So he opens the psalm with these words: 'Oh the happiness of the man whose transgression is forgiven, whose sin is covered.' He, too, found God in the darkness.

Now if this was possible in David's time, how much more possible is it today. Calvary had not happened then. But it has happened now. The blood of Christ has been shed for sinners, for the remission of sins. Redemption has been obtained at infinite cost, that the darkness of guilt might be for ever lifted from the hearts of men; that all who trust the Saviour might come right out into the glorious sunlight of God's pardoning mercy and everlasting love.

John Bunyan, in his autobiography, Grace Abounding to the Chief of Sinners, remarks: 'The guilt of sin did help me much.' We take him to mean that it was the very enormity of his sense of sin and guilt that made God's forgiveness so desirable, and, when he found it, filled his heart with such love and gratitude to God.

Jesus said much the same thing in one of His parables: 'To whom much is forgiven the same loveth much. To whom little is forgiven the same loveth little.' The depth of the darkness serves to make the dawn more beautiful. The deeper your sense of personal unworthiness the greater will be your appreciation of your Saviour's love. If God is giving you an insight unto the sinfulness of your own heart that appals you, He is marking you out for special blessing.

Isaiah was destined to become one of the greatest of the prophets. From what did his greatness spring? From an experience he had as a young man, in the year that king Uzziah died. At that time he had a vision of the temple filled with smoke. Amidst the darkness he saw the Lord sitting upon a throne, high and lifted up. He heard His glory proclaimed as the seraphim called one to another and said: 'Holy, holy, holy is the Lord of hosts; the whole earth is full of His glory.'[8]

Then Isaiah said: 'Woe is me! For I am lost; for I am a man of unclean lips, and I dwell in the midst of a people of unclean lips; for my eyes have seen the King, the Lord of hosts!'

After this he heard the voice of the Lord saying, 'Whom shall I send, and who will go for us?'

Then Isaiah said: 'Here am I! Send me.'

And the ministry which extended on beyond this point for many decades of years, derived its inspiration from this experience. Finding God in the darkness of conviction, discovering there, not only his own sinfulness but the fathomless mercy and grace of God, Isaiah went out to be God's messenger to the people of his day and age; the greatest evangelist of the Old Testament. So it can be with you.

THE DARKNESS OF DEATH

What about the last great darkness of all—the darkness of death? When we enter the valley can we hope to find God there too? Indeed we can.

The psalmist David said: 'Even though I walk through the valley of the shadow of death, I fear no evil; for Thou art with me; Thy rod and Thy staff, they comfort me.'

George Goodman was one who will be remembered by an older generation as a splendid servant of God. As an author, Bible teacher and evangelist, his labours were blessed to thousands—especially young people —many finding their way to Christ through his ministry.

His last illness was long and exceedingly distressing. After his death the following verses, composed by him during his illness, were found between the leaves of his Bible:

The reed was bruised, no music sweet
Could from the lute the player make,
It seemed as if it were more sweet
To break it and another make.

    But One in pity saw the bruise
    And smoothed it out and made it straight
    Fit for Himself again to use
    Of His great harmony partake.

O God, I am that bruised reed;
My songs of grace must almost cease;
Refit me for Thy service need,
Bring from me hymns of joy and praise.

The oil was spent within the lamp,
The flickering wick though still alight
With moistening oil was scarcely damp,
And every moment grew less bright.

>   But One stood by and saw the spark
>   Who would not quench it; but He came,
>   Lest it should fade into the dark,
>   He poured in oil, renewed the flame.

>   O God, I am that smoking flax;
>   My feeble flame is burning low;
>   Breathe on me, Spirit of the Lord
>   And cause the light once more to glow.

He led me to the way of pain—
A barren and a starless place.
(I didn't know His eyes were wet;
He wouldn't let me see His face.)

He left me like a frightened child
Unshielded in a night of storm.
(How should I dream He was so near?
The rain-swept darkness hid His form.)

But when the clouds were driven back,
And dawn was breaking into day,
I knew whose feet had walked with mine
I saw the footprints all the way.

In the end, even in his extreme desolation, he
found God in the darkness. This should be our encouragement.

WE MUST DRAW NEAR

'I could scream out for the state of helplessness I'm in!' a man said to me once. I was visiting him in a little village in one of the Welsh valleys. He was terribly crippled and in constant pain. 'God is not in this,' he said to me, 'if He were He would be the cruelest of fathers. This is just the result of the laws of nature. It has nothing to do with God.' I reasoned with him, and tried to tell him that God *was* involved with his situation, and that he could find God if he would. But it was to no purpose. Perhaps his attitude was a pathetic attempt to save God's character, in his estimation, as a God of love, but nevertheless it was a mistake. The man who adopts this attitude: 'God is not in this,' automatically precludes any possibility of finding Him.

It is written: 'Whoever would draw near to God must believe that He exists and that He rewards those who seek Him.'[10] God *is* in the darkness, and if we are to find Him, we must believe it. We must draw near in faith, trustfully, enquiringly, expectantly. If we do He will not fail us. The fact that some men have failed to find God in the darkness of their sorrows does not negate the experience of those who have —any more than the negative experience of a blind man invalidates the experience of those who have sight. Faith is the prerequisite of finding God, just as sight is a prerequisite of understanding colour.

One thing is sure: If with all your heart you truly seek Him, you shall ever surely find Him ... even though it be in thick darkness.

CHAPTER TWO

Everything Works Together

I BELIEVE in the sovereignty of God! I believe in His power to take evil in life and turn it to good! I believe this includes suffering!

Paul writes to the Christians at Rome and says: 'We know that in everything God works for good with those who love Him, who are called according to His purpose.'

From the context we learn that Paul is concerned about the problem of a world racked with pain. He catches the sound of a whole creation groaning and travailing together. In face of the boundless suffering he sees he is speechless. He knows not what to say or how to pray. The only expression he can make is in sighs too deep for words, which he trusts God interprets and understands.

But while there is so much he does not know, there is one thing he *does* know. 'We know,' he says, 'that in everything God works for good.' Of this he is certain. There is no room for doubt. However hesitant *we* may be, Paul has no hesitation whatsoever. It is axiomatic! 'This,' he says, 'we know!'

Now this is a great and glorious affirmation, of immense comfort and consolation to those who suffer —no matter what form their suffering may take. It indicates that the life of a Christian can be so divinely co-ordinated that everything tends towards one common purpose, even the most opposite and contrary events!

Just as in music, notes at either end of the scale, and chords both minor and major, combine to produce the perfect harmony, so God can use every kind of experience in the lives of His children to produce the spiritual harmony He desires.

Just as in the human body muscles working in opposition to one another keep our limbs in the desired position, so God can use the most opposite kinds of circumstances to preserve us in the way.

Just as in machinery wheels turn some clockwise and some anti-clockwise, so God can combine the contrary wheels of life to produce the ends in view.

The life of a Christian need not be a series of disconnected accidents, or disjointed happenings without rhyme or reason. It comes within the circle of the sovereignty of God. Behind each life there is a plan, and in all God does (unless we frustrate Him) He works towards its fulfilment.

NOT YOU, BUT GOD

One of the most striking examples of God working for good is provided by the life of Joseph. God's long term plan was to ensure the preservation of Jacob and his family in a time of future famine, because this family was in the line of the messianic prophecy. But what a round-about road He chose! First Joseph was favoured above his brothers! Next his brothers, in their jealousy, sold him into slavery.

After that he found himself exalted as chief steward in the house of Potiphar in sole charge of all his estate! From this enjoyable and honourable position he was thrown into prison through the perfidy of Potiphar's wife. In prison he lay out of sight and out of mind. Then Pharoah had a dream, and in next to no time Joseph found himself Prime Minister of Egypt, next only to Pharoah in authority and dignity. Addressing his trembling brothers, he said: 'Do not be distressed, or angry with yourselves, because you sold me here; for God sent me before you to preserve life ... *So it was not you who sent me here, but God!* '[2] It just had to be God!

Many centuries later Paul said '(God) set me apart before I was born.'[3] Reviewing the circumstances of his life, he too was aware of a hand that had guided and a heart that had planned. His conviction was born of the sheer facts of his experience. 'We know,' he says, 'in everything God works for good.'

EVERYTHING

Now some of us have a hard time accepting this statement as it stands. Had Paul said, 'Things work together' there would be no problem in our minds. But Paul says, 'In *everything* God works' '*All things* work together.' Not just 'things', or 'some things', or even 'many things', but '*in everything*.' This over-ruling embraces *all* the events of life, accidental or planned. There is absolutely nothing beyond its scope! It encompasses the joys of life and its sorrows, birth and death, sickness and health, failure and success, poverty and plenty, disappointment and achievement, hatred and friendship, pain and pleasure, sunshine and shadow, good and evil, weal and woe!

If we consider the specific forms of suffering discussed in the first part of this book, there is not one of them that is not included in this 'everything', this wonderful 'all'. Whether we suffer on account of our mortality, or through our involvement with others, or by our own folly, or as a discipline imposed by God, or as a test of loyalty, or vicariously, of our own free choice, or whether we suffer as a result of the combination of them all—it matters not. Whatever the reason, whatever the suffering, in God's sovereignty it can *all* be taken up and over-ruled and made to work together for good. All of it—without exceptions! This Paul affirms with a confidence nothing can shake. 'We know!' he says.

FOR GOOD

But there is another problem that has to be faced, and it is: What is meant by 'good'? We can easily accept that things work together, perhaps we can even believe that 'all things' work together—but, '*for good*'? In face of the facts of life around us how can such a statement be justified?

The answer depends on what we mean by 'good'. If we are saying, in effect, that all things work together for our profit, or for our pleasure, or for our social advancement, or for our physical well-being etc., then patently the proposition is not true. Sickness, poverty, hardship, disappointment, frustration, break-down and defeat are ingredients in the lives of Christians as much as in the lives of other persons.

These things are not excluded from our lives by the over-ruling we are speaking about.

How, then, are we to understand 'good' in this context? What is Paul talking about? He gives us the answer when he goes on to say: 'We know that in everything God works for good, with those who love Him, who are called according to His purpose. For those whom He foreknew He also predestined *to be conformed to the image of His Son,* in order that He might be the first-born among many brethren.'

The 'good' God is seeking to bring about is our conformity to Christ! His desire is that upon our lives shall be stamped the family likeness! He wants us to be known and seen to be sons of God—our Master's brethren in the household of faith! If the word 'good' carries this connotation, then our problem is solved, for there is no experience in life that cannot be made to further this end.

SPIRITUAL JUDO

One of the skills a person acquires in learning certain forms of wrestling and self-defence, is how to use the momentum of an attack and turn it to the overthrow of the attacker. A person comes lunging at you, and instead of resisting the attack by meeting it head on and hurling the attacker backwards, you accept the attack, pull him towards you faster still, and thus accelerate his progress towards a humiliating fall, while you yourself remain unhurt. So it can be in a spiritual setting.

Faced with an insult, a loveless criticism, a bitter disappointment, a financial disaster, a distressing illness, we can react towards it with resentment, and resist it to the bitter end. In doing so we may succeed in hurling back the attacker, but we ourselves can get badly hurt in the process.

On the other hand we can accept the attack, and with God-given skill turn it to our advantage, so that we come out on top in every situation. To do this is to find everything working for good. When, therefore, we are in trouble of any kind the question we should be asking is not: How can I get out of this? But: *What* can I get out of this? In so doing we shall find that there is no situation from which it is impossible to extract a blessing! We shall emerge from our troubles, not merely conquerors, but more than conquerors. That is to say, the conflict can be made to yield such benefits that when the battle is over we are left not weakened, but strengthened, not impoverished, but enriched with the spoils of victory.

This is indeed a revolutionary truth! In effect it eliminates evil from our lives by transmuting evil into good. God in His sovereignty does this again and again, and as we accept this sovereignty in our lives we can learn to do the same. Every situation which God allows a Christian to enter into is designed to make a better man of him! Holiness is achieved not by spiritual means alone, but by the rough and tumble of life. Stumbling-blocks become stepping-stones to higher and better things! We learn by our mistakes! Failure becomes the fountain of success! With a proper set of the sail and a skilful hand on the tiller even the most adverse winds of life can be made to thrust us forward.

In the light of this it is obvious, as Richard C. Halverson says in his excellent book *Between Sundays*, that 'it is not what happens to you that counts, but how you take it.'

WHY THE DIFFERENCE?

Here we come up against yet another problem, for men react to life so differently. Writing to his friends at Rome Paul said: 'We rejoice in our sufferings, knowing that suffering produces endurance, and endurance produces character, and character produces hope, and hope does not disappoint us, because God's love has been poured into our hearts through the Holy Spirit which has been given to us.'[4]

This result of suffering was certainly to be seen in Paul's life, and it has been evident in the lives of many people since. But not in everyone! We all know only too well instances where the movement has been in the opposite direction. Starting from the same point of suffering we have seen suffering producing despair, and despair producing the disintegration of character, and the disintegration of character producing disillusionment, and disillusionment producing a soul-destroying bitterness, perhaps even the complete rejection of God.

What makes the difference?

Here in each instance we have, as it were, a chain reaction sparked by suffering. In one case it moves to the right towards great benefits, and in the other case it moves to the left towards great disaster. The same difficulty that makes one man ruins another: Why?

What determines whether the chain reaction shall move to the right or to the left? Towards God or away from Him? I believe the answer is: Love—or its absence! Paul says a very significant thing: 'Suffering produces hope, and hope does not disappoint us, *because God's love has been poured into our hearts.*' Note the 'because'! This is why things happen in this way, and the chain reaction moves towards blessing—'*because*', in our suffering, God's love has been poured into our hearts.

Without a deep inward awareness of the love of God over-shadowing us in all His dealings with us, suffering can produce a soul-destroying resentment. But when this love is recognised and welcomed, suffering can produce a walk with God closer than ever. Love is the alchemy that can transmute the base metal of our trials into the solid gold of Christian character and spiritual devotion.

There are several places in Scripture where this important lesson is underlined. Paul writes to the Romans and, speaking of tribulation, distress, persecution, famine etc., says: 'In all these things we are more than conquerors through *Him who loved us.*'[5] It is through the power of that love that tribulation, persecution, poverty and peril can be so overcome that we emerge from the conflict more than conquerors. Without that love to support us, and encourage us, and take away our fears, and assure us that all is well, and give us something worth living for, we would despair. But with that love as a reality in our souls we can triumph over all.

Loved! then the way will not be drear;
For One we know is ever near,
Proving it to our hearts so clear
    That we are loved.

Time, that affects all things below,
Can never change the love He'll show;
The heart of Christ with love will flow,
    And we are loved.

Loved in the past of yesterday,
And all along our future way,
And in the present of today—
    For ever loved.

In Jude's short letter, written for Christians with the end of this age in view, we find this exhortation: 'Keep yourselves in the love of God.'[6] By this I take him to mean keep a constant awareness in your heart and mind of God's love towards you! Never let the consciousness fade! Never let familiarity breed forgetfulness!

J. B. Phillips renders it: 'Keep yourselves within the love of God.' As if the love of God were a fold and we are to shelter therein as our protection from the stormy blast. Or as if the love of God were an embrace and we are to snuggle into the cradle of those everlasting arms, for comfort in our loneliness. Or as if the love of God were a fire and we are to keep within the circle of its cheering glow. We are to keep ourselves *within* the love of God. This is essential if our suffering is to draw us nearer to God, and not drive us away from Him.

Now the question becomes: How can we do this? How *can* we keep ourselves within the love of God? By keeping close to the Cross! 'In this the love of God was made manifest among us, that God sent His only Son into the world, so that we might live through Him.'

It is easy to believe God loves us when all is plain sailing in our lives, and the zephyr breezes blow softly, but when the storms rage around us, and day is as night, and neither the sun nor moon nor stars appear, we need some other kind of assurance than that which we can derive from our circumstances. It is then we turn to the Cross.

Paul prayed that his friends at Ephesus 'may have power to comprehend with all the saints what is the breadth and length and height and depth, and to know the love of Christ which surpasses knowledge, that you may be filled with all the fullness of God'.[7] (In the Greek text 'with' is literally 'up to' all the fullness of God. What we are to be filled 'with' is the love of God.)

The final proof, demonstration and measure of God's love is found at Calvary! That love is poured into our hearts by the Holy Spirit as we begin to understand the meaning of Calvary.

God is love. I feel it in the air around me;
God is love. I read it in the heavens above me;
God is love. All nature doth agree;
But the greatest proof of His love to me
Is Calvary.

One thing more, however, remains to be said: If our suffering is to work as God intends, for good, then God's love for us must be matched by our love for Him, together with an acceptance of His will for our lives.

Paul says: 'In everything God works for good with those that love Him, who are called according to His purpose.' If we do not love God, if we have not come to agreement with Him about what He wants to do in our lives, the good He intends will not seem good to us. The promise is qualified!

Paul's words of assurance are for Christians only! Particularly for those Christians who truly love God and earnestly desire to see His purpose fulfilled in their lives. How important, therefore, that you search your heart about this matter, if you wish to experience this divine over-ruling in your affairs. Do you *really* love God? With all your heart?

Can you honestly say with Peter: 'Lord, You know everything; You know that I love You.'[8] Is it the deepest longing of your heart to be conformed to the likeness of your Master and Lord?

> Impress Thine image on me;
> Dear Lord, I would obey!
> Be Thou the skilful potter,
> And I the yielded clay.
> Mold me, Oh, mold me to Thy will,
> While in Thy hand I'm lying still.

Is this your constant prayer? If so, you qualify for this triumphant, God-ordered life. If not? Well, perhaps now is the time to get in line, for, believe me, there is no life on earth so thrilling or so utterly secure as that life in which God works in everything for good.

CHAPTER THREE

Facing Death

'IS NOT THE fear of death natural to man, sir?' The question was put by James Boswell to the celebrated Dr. Johnson. His reply: 'So much so that the whole of life is simply the putting away of the thought of it!'

But we cannot put away the thought of it for ever. Sooner or later we have to confront it as it comes either to those near and dear to us, or to ourselves.

Of all the preachers I have listened to throughout the years no one charmed or delighted me more than Dinsdale T. Young, for so long the valiant and venerable occupant of the pulpit of the Methodist Central Hall, Westminster. How well I remember one occasion when he leaned his patriarchal head over the pulpit Bible, gathered us all together in a sweeping glance, paused a moment, and then, in his rich, sonorous voice said: 'Man, when you come to die remember that your dying is the last thing you can do for your Lord down here. Mind you do it well, for if you don't you can't come back and do it again.'

Through the years since those words have lived with me. I hope I remember them when my time comes.

A valued colleague in the London Baptist ministry,

Leslie Larwood, before his death, made an appeal to the members of his congregation for frankness, honesty and confidence between members of the family when faced with the terminal illness of a loved one.

It arose out of his own experience when told by his doctor that he had no more than two weeks, at the most, to live. The information was shared with his wife and family, and this they found to be such a blessing that he wished that all who find themselves in a similar situation might do the same.

He described the help they found in being able to be completely open with one another. He could discuss and settle to his satisfaction business and domestic matters. His doctor was much better able to prepare him for the final hours and ease his passing. A minister friend was able to speak to him freely and minister Christ to him without embarrassment or reserve. But above all he experienced such a depth of fellowship with his loved ones, such a release of tension, an inward tranquility, such a sense of God's presence as made those days of waiting infinitely precious. In a final tape recorded message to his people, he told of his experience. He spoke of the charades which so often take place in the sick room when every possible evasion and deception is used to avoid facing the unwelcome fact that the end of the road is fast approaching. He spoke of the barrier to communication and a personal ministry of help and comfort that such an attitude has so often been, and pleaded for a more truly Christian stance in face of death.

It was a remarkable and moving message, spoken with all the sincerity that belongs to those moments when nothing earthly matters any more. And it went to the heart of a very real, indeed, a universal human problem—how to face death.

It is understandable that those without Christian faith should shrink from the final reality—though it must be said that sometimes they face it with a fortitude which puts some Christians to shame—but that Christians should cringe and seek refuge in unreality seems to me to be a craven denial of the faith.

Paul writes to the Corinthians and says: 'All things are yours, whether ... the world or life *or death* or the present or the future, all are yours; and you are Christ's; and Christ is God's.'[1] Death is one of God's gifts to His children. To the man of God it ceases to be a curse and becomes a blessing, a golden opportunity of serving the Master.

What shape or form that opportunity will take no one can tell until the time comes.

How well I remember another sermonic feast I enjoyed from the lips of Dinsdale Young. He preached one Sunday on the words of Moses to Pharoah: 'We do not know with what we must serve the Lord until we arrive there.'[2] We need to be prepared for all eventualities, and never more so than in relation to our final hours on earth.

Some of us when we come to the river find we have to contend with all the swellings of Jordan, others pass over almost dry shod. Some are taken without a moments warning, with no time for reflection, others have all the time in the world as life drags

on through months and years of weariness and pain.
Some retain their mental faculties till their very last
breath, others drift imperceptibly into a senility
which makes rational communication impossible
long before they pass away. Some die in loneliness,
with no one near to help, others have a friend to
hold their hand all the way through the valley. Some
die in harness in the full vigour of their life, others
live till second childhood overtakes them and they
have to be cared for once again like babies. We
simply cannot forsee the future or know with what
we shall be required to serve the Lord until we come
thither. Only one thing we do know—there will be
some way in which we can serve Him, and we ought
to do it well.

One thing has disturbed me on a number of occasions over the years of my ministry: the way in
which some earnest Christian people lose the opportunity of serving their Lord in this way, through a
refusal to recognise that their time has come, and an
importunate prayer for recovery, when it is as certain as human judgment can determine that no recovery is going to take place. I have heard people
say: 'Doctor, I know I am going to get better, God
has told me so,' when the doctor knew perfectly well,
and events proved, that no recovery was possible. I
have often wondered what the reaction of a non-
Christian doctor might be to 'faith' of that kind. It
seems to me he must find it less than impressive, to
say the least. But when a patient says: 'Doctor, if it
proves to be as you say, that my days are numbered,
I want you to know that I accept that verdict with

perfect peace in my heart. God will see me through', then I think the doctor would be very impressed indeed.

I know it cannot be easy to accept the inevitable, and there are some who make it much harder for the sufferer than it need be. A person who has been ill for a long time with a distressing complaint can frequently find himself a prey for all sorts of cranks and quacks, religious and otherwise—well-meaning, but misguided persons with their particular axe to grind. Anonymous letters, phone calls from complete strangers, callers at the house, all offering counsel and help—sometimes in a most persistent way— are familiar experiences. It is not to be wondered at that in their weakness and desperation people who are very ill grasp at these offers—but for all that we need to remember that they can lead to happenings that are far from glorifying to God or helpful to the sufferer.

One of the most distressing scenes I have ever witnessed occurred in a hospital room where a valiant servant of God lay dying. At the end of a long and most painful illness events proved that she had only a matter of hours to live. There was scarcely a breath in her poor, broken body and she was completely unconscious. While she was in this state some four or five men entered the room, distributed themselves around the bed, fell on their knees, laid their hands on the dying woman and began to claim her restoration. Praying loudly and passionately, pleading the blood of Jesus; giving thanks that they could already feel the healing flowing through her veins and that

she was slowly recovering; amidst fervent 'Halle-
lujahs', they 'prayed the prayer of faith' and
'believed' for her complete restoration. I shall never
forget the scene as long as memory holds. I hung my
head in shame at such an utter contradiction of the
faith we profess. They couldn't have pleaded for my
friend's recovery more insistently if she had been on
the brink of hell, instead of on the verge of heaven.
Are we not pilgrims and strangers down here? Is it
not written that we seek a city which is to come?

Did not Jesus say: 'I have a home prepared for
you?'

Did not Paul write: 'I have a desire to depart and
to be with Christ which is far better ... to die is
gain'?

The hospital staff surrounding my friend were all
unbelievers. Can we imagine they were drawn closer
to Christ by what they too witnessed that day? Fortunately my friend knew nothing of what was happening, but taking the total picture is this doing our
dying well?

Contrast this scene with another which also took
place in hospital. A lady who had been converted to
Christ late in life, and only a few years before this
happening, was stricken with cancer and was told
that she had only a few months to live. She accepted
the verdict courageously and calmly, with perfect
confidence in the will of God for her future. One
evening, reading her Bible as she lay in bed, a neigh-
bouring patient enquired what she was reading and
asked if she would read aloud. This she did. A day or
two afterwards she was asked if she would offer a

prayer. Before long, at the request of the patients in
that large ward, she was taking evening prayers
every day. This she did until weakness overcame
her and made it impossible. Finally she died. But
what a testimony! How well she served her Lord
in her dying hours—and she had been a Christian for
only a very few years.

In Alexander Gammie's life of D. J. Findlay, of
Glasgow, he tells of a letter received by Findlay from
Dr F. B. Meyer, of saintly memory. It was written
three days before Meyer's death. This is what it said:
'My dear F. and wife,—To my surprise I have just
been told that my days and hours are numbered. It
may be that before this reaches you I shall have gone
into the Palace. Don't trouble to write. We shall
meet in the morning.—With much love, Yours affec-
tionately, F. B. Meyer.' I think any man who can
write like that is doing his dying well.

John Wesley used to say: Our people die well.
Among those early Methodist folk the hope of eternal
life was real and strong. So it should be with us today. I think the trouble with some of us is that we
don't really believe in eternal life. We have so set
our hearts on things of earth, and we have so failed to
set our affections on things above, that we have forgotten that our citizenship is in heaven.

MASKING DEATH

There are three basic attitudes that can be adopted
towards death—we can, for instance, endeavour to
ignore it.

History tells that in the days of the French revolu-

tion, The Bastille, along with the other prisons of
Paris, was filled with the hated aristocrats. Within
its walls the prisoners endeavoured to keep up their
spirits by acting as if nothing had altered. They ex-
changed their accustomed courtesies, they bowed to
one another, did the polite thing and engaged in their
usual pleasantries. Each night a jailer came round
and put a red mark over certain cell doors. Next
morning all within that cell were bundled into the
tumbrils and taken away to the scaffold. It is said
they kept up this mockery to the very last man.

The same attitude is easily recognisable today. It
is an ostrich-like stance, and it was never easier to
adopt than at the present time.

Then we can attempt to conceal the grim realities.
Death has been very largely taken out of our homes
and removed to the remoteness of a hospital ward.
We can go many years without encountering it at
close quarters. Funeral customs on the North Ameri-
can continent, for instance, are a blatant example of
concealing death, designed as they are to do everything imaginable to distract the mind from reality.
Heavy embalming; the lavish use of cosmetics so that
the deceased 'looks beautiful'; plastic surgery to restore the facial appearance of someone killed and
injured in an accident; the adornment of the corpse
with all the trappings of life—a new suit or dress,
the accustomed jewellery and ornaments, even to
wearing spectacles! Elaborate caskets lined with bil-
lowing cushions of the brightest colours; all conspire
to mask the ugly realities of dissolution, and make a
visit to the funeral parlour to pay one's respects, and

view the deceased, an event completely devoid of shock. So unreal can it be, that, except for those closely concerned, it can become quite meaningless.

Such are the costly and elaborate efforts we make in our Western world as we seek to conceal death and contrive ways of putting it out of mind.

NOT ALL SUCCEED

Some people, however, find it impossible either to forget or to conceal death. The Bible speaks about those 'who through fear of death were subject to life-long bondage'.[3] There are many such, perhaps more than we realise, for few care to admit to their feelings or talk about their fears. While these pages were being written a great Toronto daily paper devoted one whole front page to these matters, under the caption, COPING WITH DEATH. Some of the city's leading doctors and psychiatrists were interviewed and asked for their opinions about the state of mind of people with reference to death.

Their replies were illuminating. A leading psychiatrist at a Toronto hospital, said: 'We are a youth-orientated people. We want to be young looking all the time. We go for plastic surgery and then transplants because we never want to die . . . Fear of death and efforts to avoid it are major features of our culture, and doctors are caught in the middle because we reflect the people who want us to fight tooth and nail to avoid it.'

A consultant psychiatrist gave his opinion: 'People die afraid and feeling unloved. Relatives are alone and bitter. They have never faced death in life or talked with their loved ones about what illness or death means. And it is all caused by our fear.'

A teacher of nursing, said: 'Nurses still come to me shattered (by death). They've avoided death all their lives. They've discussed it in class, but in a detached way, and to see someone die is so different. The nurses often try to substitute action for compassion. They call the morgue, they run and get coffee for the relatives. But they don't talk to the dying, or face the concepts of death for themselves.'

Said another: 'We mess up death with our denials.' Along with all this, medical technology (with its endless assortment of tubes, pumps, suckers, machines and spare parts taken from other people) exerts itself day and night to stave off the dreaded moment of death (spending thousands of pounds in the process) even though the person concerned may have little or nothing to live for.

So Boswell was right and Dr. Johnson gave the correct answer. We might as well admit it!

But there is a third option: that provided by the Christian gospel. Jesus, we are told, came *to deliver* those who through fear of death are all their life-time subject to bondage. There is a deliverance from this fear which does not have to be gained by escaping into unreality, but is to be obtained by faith.

In the newspaper article referred to, some of the doctors attributed the increasing fear of death in our society to the explosion of the 'Christian myth'. I would not put it that way, though I would say it might be due to the decay of Christian faith. We can accept the back-handed acknowledgement that

FACING DEATH 101

Christian faith destroys the fear of death, but we reject the notion that it is a myth. We affirm that we have adequate reasons for faith. We have not followed cunningly devised fable, or old wives' tales. The historical events upon which our faith is based were not done in a corner. We feel solid ground beneath our feet. It is so true, however, that once we turn away from Christ there is nothing left for us but fear.

On one occasion Jesus was faced with the defection of a large number of His followers. Turning to His disciples He said: 'Will you also go away?' Peter answered: 'Lord, to whom shall we go? You have the words of eternal life.'[4]

Jesus Christ our Lord, by His glorious resurrection that first Easter day, brought life and immortality to light, and when He is welcomed and His gospel believed, the shadows that surround the grave disappear. But when we reject the gospel there is no alternative in face of death but hopelessness and fear.

'In my experience,' said one of the psychiatrists reported in the newspaper, 'I have never seen (death accepted with) bland peace.'

Poor man! In my experience I have seen it times without number. But I suppose those who have found deliverance from the fear of death through Jesus would not need the psychiatrist's services, so he would not come across them. To his great loss!

THE CONCLUSION OF THE MATTER
What, then, is the conclusion of this matter to be? Firstly, that we make sure beyond all doubt and

question that our feet are firmly planted on the Rock of Ages, that our whole reliance is on Christ and that we know where we are going. While there is one tiny scrap of dependence upon our own goodness, respectability, or religiousness, we cannot be sure. Certainty comes only when we depend *wholly* on Christ.

> Upon a life I did not live;
> Upon a death I did not die:
> Another's life; another's death;
> I rest my whole eternity.

'My brother,' said the beloved Dr. Young, 'when you come to die, mind you die on justification. Don't you die on sanctification. Die on justification. Die on the merits of Jesus' blood.' They were wise words.

It has been said that when Bishop James Butler, author of the celebrated *Analogy of Religion*, lay dying, he experienced a period of doubt and uncertainty. To his curate, at his bedside, he said words to this effect: 'All the sermons I have preached, the books I have written and the things I have said, bring me no comfort now!'

His curate replied: 'My lord, have you forgotten that Jesus Christ is a saviour *for sinners?*'

'No,' breathed the bishop, 'I haven't. But how may I know He is a saviour *for me?*'

'My lord,' said his curate, 'have you forgotten that Jesus said: "Him who comes to me I will not cast out"?'[5]

'Ah!' said the bishop, 'that's it.'

Yes, indeed. That's it. Once we are sure that we belong to Christ we need have no fear of death, no matter when or how it may strike.

The next thing to do is to be busy about the Master's business; occupying, as He puts it, until He comes.

> Not many lives, but only *one* have we,
> One only one;
> How sacred should that one life be,
> That narrow span.
> Day after day filled up with blessed toil,
> Hour after hour still bringing in new spoil.
> Horatious Bonar.

The last thing to remember is: When we are finally confronted by death let us make sure that we face it with complete candour, and, in the measure in which we may have opportunity, let us determine to do our dying well. If we have fears, expose them to the promises of God. The words spoken to Israel, so long ago, have their application to every person who belongs to Christ: 'Fear not, for I have redeemed you; I have called you by name, you are mine. When you pass through the waters I will be with you; and through the rivers, they shall not overwhelm you ... For I am the Lord your God, the Holy One of Israel, your Saviour.'[6]

And again: 'For I, the Lord your God, hold your right hand; it is I who say to you, "Fear not, I will help you." '[7] With help like this at hand, who need falter?

CHAPTER FOUR

The Ultimate Prayer

OCCASIONS ARISE in life when we become aware that nothing is going to prevent the hand of unspeakable tragedy from falling upon us. Prayers for deliverance offer no hope. The die has been cast. Our worst fears have been confirmed, and now nothing can stay their execution.

At such times what shall a Christian say? How shall he pray? When prayers for deliverance are no longer appropriate, and such words are empty of meaning, what shall he ask for? What is the ultimate prayer? That we should have an answer is important, for we may arrive at such a point in our lives at any time.

The answer to these questions is in an incident in the life of our Lord recorded in John's Gospel, chapter 12.

Jesus had come close to the end of His earthly ministry. One day Andrew and Philip brought word that certain Greeks wanted to see Him and talk with Him. The announcement was significant.

At the time of Jesus' birth wise men had come seeking Him, from the East—now, at the close of His ministry men come from the West. They represented uncounted millions of Gentile believers destined to be harvested in the centuries which were to follow. As Jesus heard the news trouble filled His soul. Catching a vision of the harvest, He caught, at the same time a vision of the sowing that must precede the harvest, and of Himself as the seed. 'Unless a grain of wheat falls into the earth and dies, it remains alone;' He said, 'but if it dies it bears much fruit.'[1]

He knew His hour had come; death was inevitable; nothing could save Him now. His instinct was to pray. Listen to what He said: 'Now is my soul troubled. And what shall I say? "Father, save me from this hour"? No, for this purpose I have come to this hour. *Father, glorify Thy name.*'[2]

Here, then, we have the answer we are seeking. This is what to say when we reach our moment of destiny: 'Father, glorify Thy name.'

WHAT SHALL I SAY

It is comforting to us in our frailty to know that even our Lord Christ could find Himself nonplussed. So often at such times we think we are the only ones to have such an experience, and we grow discouraged in consequence. Now we can take heart. We do not have as our friend and helper one who cannot be touched with a feeling of our infirmities. He faced the same situations as we face, and because He overcame we can come with confidence and find help in our time of need. He knows our problem and understands our thoughts exactly.

As Jesus faced all that lay before Him, His first thought was: 'Father, save me from this hour.' It was His immediate, spontaneous and human re-action.

Some Bible expositors, however, take exception to this interpretation. They regard such a thought as evidence of weakness. To them any suggestion that Jesus shrank from the Cross appears unworthy. They consider the sentence should be constructed as a question: 'What shall I say? Father, save me from this hour?' In their view it was just a passing thought immediately thrown out.

But their scruples are unnecessary. We need to remember that our Lord was unique in His person in that he possessed the divine nature and the human, and these two constantly pressed upon Him. Here we see the human side of His nature reacting to the situation with an altogether human cry of dismay: 'Father, save me from this hour!'

Had Jesus not shrunk from the Cross could we have regarded Him as human at all? Jesus was no stoic; and we are not expected to be stoics either. If sometimes in our anguish we cry out, Father, save me from this hour ... spare me *this* ... anything Lord, but *this* ... He understands. We need not fear that we are offending. He knows our frame and re-members that we are dust. There is only so much any of us can take, and He knows when the breaking point has been reached.

BUT ...

Having cried out for deliverance Jesus immedi-ately realised that this would not do. 'But for this purpose I have come to this hour,' He said. As if to say: I was born for this hour; all my life I have been moving towards it; how can I refuse it now that it has come? The whole purpose of my life has been to take this cup into my hands. Why have I placed it to my lips if I don't intend to drink? He can no longer pray: 'Father, save me from this hour.' The words will not fit the situation. The Cross is inescapable.

Many times in the lives of men and women such a moment of truth arrives. It can come as it came to many of those Congo missionaries during the terrible months of the Simba risings, when whole families were wiped out without mercy. What can a man say, how can he pray when he has watched his wife and children murdered in cold blood and knows he is to be the next victim? It comes when a man is told he will never work again ... when we are faced with inevitable financial disaster ... at the breaking up of a long-loved home ... when we realise our cherished ambition will never be achieved, nor some coveted friendship granted ... as we hear the dreadful news that someone we dearly love is to be taken from us ... when we learn that we ourselves have reached the end of the road and that our days are numbered ... at such times we come to our moment of truth. The time for praying for deliverance has passed! The cup is touching our lips! It only remains for us to drink it to the dregs!

We have to remember that sometimes God's will is to deliver us, not by saving us *from* the dark valley, but by taking us through it to the light that shines beyond.

At such times only one prayer will fit: 'Father,

glorify Thy name!' It was the prayer our Master prayed, and it will do for us!

WHAT IS GOD'S NAME?

But what is God's name, and what is the real meaning of this prayer?

By God's name is meant His character, viewed as a whole, as that character has been revealed to men. A name describes the character of a thing. Tell me the name of that piece of wood and I will tell its qualities. Tell me the name of that engine and I will tell you it's type and it's potential. God's name stands for Himself. When God commissioned Moses to lead the Children of Israel out of Egypt into Canaan, Moses was concerned that he should be able to tell the people the name of the One who had spoken to him. 'If I come to the people of Israel and say to them, "The God of your fathers has sent me to you," and they ask me, "What is His name?" What shall I say to them?'[3]

And God said to Moses: 'I am who I am.' And He said, 'Say this to the people of Israel, "I AM hath sent me to you." ' A strange name indeed. But what other could He give? For God to say, 'My name is Father,' might obscure the fact that God is also judge. To say, 'My name is Love,' might cloud the fact that God is also light. To say, 'I am a consuming fire,' might hide the fact that God is also merciful and gracious. For God to say I AM *any one thing in particular*, might conceal the rest of His attributes. Friend, Saviour, Judge, Eternal, Lord: each of these is *a* name of God, but none of them is *His name*. In effect God said to

Moses: 'My name is Myself—all that I am in the fullness of My being, and character, and eternity. You ask Me My name—who I am? What can I say? How can I put it all into words? *I AM WHO I AM.*'

In praying: 'Father, glorify Thy name,' Our Lord, therefore, was asking that the character of God might be glorified in every aspect of the sombre events that lay ahead of Him.

And His prayer was answered. A voice came from heaven, 'I have glorified it, and I will glorify it again.'

How was God's name glorified? In the very praying of the prayer. When at such a moment of final crisis a man's thoughts turn away from himself to God, desiring God's glory only, God is glorified in that very desire. His character is enhanced. He is glorified in the devotion, submission and utter trust that inspire the prayer; in the absence of complaint, bitterness and despair; in the serenity and calm which the prayer breathes; in the supreme faith it expresses that despite all appearances God remains in control of everything.

It was glorified further in the course of subsequent events, for in the end all turned out well. Earth's saddest day was followed, three days later, by earth's gladdest day. The tragedy of the crucifixion gave place to the glory of the resurrection. Death was swallowed up in victory. The Cross proved to be the way to the Crown. God was glorified in the way in which He turned evil into good. Of all the senseless things that ever happened the killing of Jesus of Nazareth must have seemed the worst. Yet in the sovereignty of God this crime was taken up in a

purpose of redemption for mankind which could not
have been accomplished in any other way. God made
the wrath of man to praise Him, and in so doing was
glorified.

When, therefore, in my moment of extremity and
utter desperation I pray: 'Father, glorify Thy name,'
I am asking that God will so strengthen and enable
me personally, and so over-rule the course of events,
that everything that takes place shall contribute to
the glory of His name, that is, the enhancement of
His character.

There is no higher level of prayer than this; no
prayer more noble, more far reaching, more fitting,
more truly in the name of Christ. This is the ultimate
prayer. It will always be answered.

So if Himself He come to thee,
And stand before thee,
Gazing down on thee with eyes that smile and suffer,
And reach to thee Himself the Holy cup,
Pallid and royal,
Saying, Drink with Me.
Wilt thou refuse?
Nay. Not for paradise.
Hold fast His hand though the nails pierce thine too.

CHAPTER FIVE

For the Third Time: No!

GOD ALWAYS reserves the right to say, No! We shall
never properly understand the right use of prayer
unless we recognise this fact, and are in agreement
with it. On some matters God has clearly indicated
His pleasure in specific promises, and in these instances we can pray with confidence that we shall
surely have the thing we have desired. The promises
of salvation belong to this category.

> 'If I ask Him to receive me
> Will He say me nay?
> Not till earth and not till heaven
> Pass away!'

Christ has promised: 'Him who comes to Me I will
not cast out.'[1] That word never will—never can be
broken! But on other matters God's promises are
couched in general terms which may, or may not
apply to one's own particular case. In these instances
we must always be prepared for Him to say, No!

How are we to know when this *is* His answer? In
prayers for recovery from illness, for example, when
it seems recovery is not to be granted, how are we
to discern when God has finally said, No? When

should we stop praying for recovery and begin praying for strength to live with our limitations? These
are questions of wide-spread concern and deep consequence. It is important we do not give up too
easily, for the will to live and the hope of ultimately
throwing off our disability, whatever it may be, is a
major part of the healing process, as we all recognise.
Amazing recoveries have taken place in people who
have simply refused to give up and have fought their
disabilities until at last they have quite overcome
them. Yet at the same time it is equally important
that we do not waste in a useless struggle against the
inevitable, strength which could be conserved and
used in more productive and positive ways. This
happens all too often, and much has been lost in
consequence which would have been of great value
to those concerned.

PAUL'S THORN

The case of Paul the apostle brings these issues
right out into the open, and pours a flood of light on
them.

He tells of his experience: 'To keep me from being
too elated by the abundance of revelations, a thorn
was given me in the flesh, a messenger of Satan, to
harass me, to keep me from being too elated. Three
times I besought the Lord about this, that it should
leave me; but He said to me, "My grace is sufficient
for you, for My power is made perfect in weakness."
I will all the more gladly boast of my weaknesses,
that the power of Christ may rest upon me ... when
I am weak, then I am strong.'[2] This is an interesting

passage and there is much we can learn from it.

One thing is clear: Paul's words completely destroy the notion that sickness or infirmity in a Christian is always contrary to God's will, and that its continuance indicates some spiritual deficiency on the part of the sufferer.

We do not know what was the nature of the 'thorn in the flesh,' and it is idle to speculate. What is beyond doubt is that it was a physical condition which Paul found humiliating, and which tended to incapacitate him for the work he wanted to do for his Lord and Master. It left him constantly 'weak'.

It is also clear this physical infirmity was 'given' him (such is the word he uses) by the Lord. When this happened we do not know. The trouble may have been congenital. Or it may have been a complaint he contracted at a certain point in the course of his ministry, perhaps as a result of the hardships he endured. Probably the latter alternative is correct, since he speaks of his trouble as 'Satan's messenger', which might indicate he received it through some Satanic attack, either directly or indirectly upon his person.

But the point he makes is: even if Satan was the 'messenger' who brought the trouble, *it was God who sent it*! And it was from God's hand that Paul accepted it.

If, therefore, God can send sickness or physical infirmity into the lives of His servants, for their good, we can no longer hold, as some do, that perfect physical health must be the will of God for all His people, and that failure to attain this indicates some lack of faith or obedience on their part. This common application of the notion that healing is in the atonement will not stand up to the clear testimony of this passage—unless, of course, we hold Paul to be mistaken.

Concerning his problem Paul prayed. He prayed earnestly. He 'besought' the Lord. His was not a casual prayer, but an agonising prayer.

He 'implored' the Lord (such is the force of the Greek text). This he did once, but the complaint was not removed from him. A second time he begged that it might leave him, but to no avail. A third time he asked, and for the third time God said, No.

At this point Paul accepted his disability as being what in fact it was, a gift given him by the Lord for a specific and adequate reason—to keep him constantly dependent upon a strength other than his own, and to keep him always humble before God and men.

But Paul did not give up hope easily, or accept his condition as inevitable without a struggle. He did not take the first denial as a final answer—he might have misinterpreted its meaning. So he implored God a second time, and a third time. But when for the third time, God said, No, Paul knew in his spirit that he was not mistaken; the Lord had spoken, and quite clearly it was not His intention that Paul should be healed.

This is How

Now I believe this is the only way any of us in similar circumstances, can know what is God's will for us. I believe it is right for us to ask that the irksome trouble might be removed; to ask for healing, for instance, if this is what we need. I believe it is right for us even to 'implore' God, and to do so again and again if the answer is apparently denied. But I also believe we must be prepared in every instance to arrive at the point where God says: 'For the third time: No.' How do we know when we have reached that point and heard this final verdict? I cannot say. The matter is altogether too complex and personal. I believe we just *know*!

One of God's honoured servants, whom I knew well, contracted cancer. For a long time he fought hard against the inevitable. Because he was trying to get better he was constantly over-reaching himself and fretting at his inability to do all the things he thought he should be doing. For him and for those loved ones surrounding him life was an almost unbearable strain. The atmosphere in his room held a tension that could be felt by anyone entering it.

Then one day he heard the Lord say, No! so plainly that there was no mistaking His meaning. He accepted the verdict and resigned himself to his limitations. His whole attitude to his illness changed. He became calm and radiant—even jocular. Those who visited him found his room to be like an ante-chamber of heaven, just filled with the gracious presence of the Lord. And so it continued right to the day when splendidly and triumphantly he crossed the river.

He had conceded God's right to say, No!

GRACE ENOUGH

The kind of experience I have just described is common to Christian and non-Christian alike. It is

widely recognised that when a person hears that
some inevitable disaster looms ahead, or his days are
numbered there often follows a period of frantic
struggle followed by resignation to the inevitable.

But between the Christian and the non-Christian
there is a vital difference.

Throughout this experience the Christian has resources to draw upon of which the non-Christian
knows nothing. All *he* has to fall back on are whatever resources he can muster within himself, or
gather from his friends. But the Christian has available to him the inexhaustible fullness of God. 'My
grace,' said the Lord to His servant, 'is sufficient for
thee.' God's grace meaning, quite simply, God's help.

There are two ways in which my aching arm can
be eased of a tiring load: one is to remove the burden, the other for someone else to put his arm under
mine. When God says, No, to removing the load He
never does so without offering us His arm to lean
upon. His help is available, and it will prove more
than adequate.

So Paul rejoices in the denial of his prayer. His
attitude towards his affliction changes fundamen-
tally. No longer does he view it as a handicap, now he
sees it as an asset; a blessing in disguise! Now he
meets it not with resignation but with cheers. What
before brought him a sense of inferiority and humiliation is now a theme of 'boasting'. Amazing transfor-
mation! 'I will all the more gladly boast of my weakness, that the power of Christ may rest upon me . . .
when I am weak, then am I strong.'

The Lord said, No! But out of that denial came an

unimaginable gain in usefulness and effectiveness of ministry.

So it was with Paul. So it has been in thousands of instances since. So it can be again.

THE WEAVER

My life is but a weaving
　　Between my Lord and me;
I cannot choose the colours,
　　He worketh steadily.

Oft-times He weaveth sorrow,
　　And I, in foolish pride
Forget He sees the upper,
　　And I the under side.

Not till the loom is silent
　　And the shuttles cease to fly,
Shall God unroll the canvas
　　And explain the reason why.

The dark threads are as needful,
　　In the Weaver's skilful hand,
As the threads of gold and silver
　　In the pattern he has planned.

He knows, He loves, He cares—
　　Nothing this truth can dim;
He gives the very best to those,
　　Who leave the choice with Him.
　　　　　　　　Origin unknown

CHAPTER SIX

By Faith!

A PAIR of chemist's balances are excellent for weighing grammes and milligrammes, and the findings may be accurate, but they are useless for weighing bags of coal. Such delicate balances are not made for the job.

So it is with these finite minds of ours. They can work astonishingly well as long as they restrict themselves to weighing finite matters (though even in this respect they cannot always be depended on, because, weighing the same issues, one man's findings often differ from another man's findings—so there must be something wrong somewhere!). But when called upon to weigh *infinite* matters we find no one can cope.

Reason is God's wonderful gift to man. Among other things it elevates him away above the brute creation. Upon it man constantly depends, for without it he has not even instinct to guide him. He becomes utterly and pitifully lost.

But even reason has limits beyond which it cannot travel; boundaries where it has to yield up its leadership to faith. These are reached when we confront the infinite. Never is this more true than in relation to the problem of infinite suffering.

In the letter to the Hebrews we find these words:
'By faith we understand.'[1] A significant statement. It
is the ultimate answer to our quest!

When all is said and done, and every argument has
been advanced, there are still instances and aspects of
suffering which defy satisfactory explanation on
purely rational grounds. We are cast back upon faith
if we are to understand.

FAITH IS NOT BLIND

The faith we are speaking of is not a nebulous
faith: a kind of feeling that someone, somewhere in
the great beyond is somehow or other in charge. Nor
is it a blind faith, operating without rhyme or reason.
It is faith in a person whom we know we can trust
to the hilt.

When the temple police, led by Judas, the be-
trayer, arrived to take Jesus captive, Peter resisted,
but Jesus stopped him, saying: 'Shall I not drink the
cup which *the Father has given me?*'[2] A cup held in
the Father's hand could be offered only in love! However bitter its contents it must be safe to drink.

A father takes a dearly-loved child to hospital.
There his little boy has to undergo most painful tests.
The lad is not old enough to have the meaning of it
all explained to him, he is not capable of understanding. The only understanding open to him is that
which comes through faith in his father's love and
wisdom. And until he grows older and is at last able
to learn what happened to him, and why, this has to
suffice.

So it is with us. Sometimes we can be given the explanations; sometimes we cannot. When we cannot we have to be content to understand by faith!

THE GOOD WAY

From a number of points of view this is a good way to understand. For one thing, it brings understanding within the reach of all.

The Bible speaks about the poor in this world who are *rich in faith*. If the solution to life's problems could be appreciated only by the intellectuals the vast bulk of human beings would be left in the dark. We are not all capable of logic, but we are all capable of faith. Every rational person exercises faith every time he puts his foot to the ground.

Also, faith opens our eyes to things we should not otherwise be able to see. Reason can see a long way, but faith can see further. Reason may be a pair of spectacles; faith is a telescope.

Says Paul: 'What no eye has seen, nor ear heard, nor the heart of man conceived, what God has prepared for those who love Him, God has revealed to us through the Spirit.'[3] These things we apprehend by faith.

Faith teaches humility, and it is to humble minds and hearts that God makes known His secrets. Human reason, like the rest of our being, is corrupted by man's moral and spiritual fall. Nowhere is this fact more apparent, or this corruption more complete, than when reason exalts itself above God and presumes to know better than He how this world should be run. 'The world,' we are told, 'did not know God *through wisdom*.'[4]

On one occasion Jesus said: 'I thank Thee, Father, Lord of heaven and earth, that Thou hast hidden these things from the wise and understanding and revealed them to babes; yea, Father, for such was Thy gracious will.'[5]

God's secrets revealed not to professors but to babes! Why so? Because there is no barrier to learning God's secrets more effective than pride, and no way more open than humility. Humility. More humility. Much humility! This is the way faith leads us to an understanding of what God is doing in His dealings with His children. Precept upon precept, line upon line, here a little and there a little, is how God teaches us—if we are believing enough and humble enough to learn. And faith, when it is acted on, leads to the certainty of experience: 'Nothing before; nothing behind; the step of faith falls on the seeming void—to find the rock beneath.'

The understanding which comes through faith is solid and substantial.

LEARN GOD'S CHARACTER

'He knows the way that I take; when He has tried me, I shall come forth as gold.'[6] So said Job in the midst of his suffering. He spoke the language of faith. For his assurance that all was well he did not depend on having all the answers, he depended on the character of God!

Said one theological professor of a former age to

his studens, using the quaint language of those days:
'My dears! Learn the attributes of God, and then lean
on Him.'

His advice could not be bettered!

SUMMARY OF PART TWO, AND PERSONAL CHECK

In face of personal suffering have I learned:

	YES	NO
1. To believe that God is with me, even in the darkness, and am I seeking Him there? See Chapter One.		
2. That God is working for good in every area of my life? See Chapter Two.		
3. To look on death as a golden opportunity of serving the Master? See Chapter Three.		
4. To seek God's glory above everything else? See Chapter Four.		
5. To concede God's right to say, No, to my desires? See Chapter Five.		
6. To commit everything in faith into a loving Father's hands, and leave it there? See Chapter Six.		

Bible References

Revised Standard Version, unless otherwise indicated.

PART I

Chapter 1

1. Job 10:2
2. 1 Cor. 13:12

Chapter 2

1. 1 Sam. 25:29 AV
2. 1 Cor. 12:26
3. Job 5:7
4. Deut. 5:9
5. Deut. 5:9, 10

Chapter 3

1. Heb. 2:2
2. 2 Thess. 1:6
3. Heb. 2:2, 3
4. Rom. 2:5, 6
5. Num. 32:23
6. Gal. 6:7, 8
7. Heb. 9:27
8. Gen. 15:16
9. Ex. 34:6
10. Isa. 53:5–6
11. 1 Pet. 2:24
12. 2 Sam. 12:13, 14
13. Ps. 32:10
14. Luke 23:39

Chapter 4

1. Heb. 12:6, 7
2. Jer. 48:11 NEB
3. Luke 22:32
4. Luke 22:33
5. Matt. 26:33, 35
6. Heb. 12:10, 11
7. Rom. 5:3–5
8. Jas. 1:2, 3
9. 2 Cor. 1:3, 4
10. Heb. 2:10

Chapter 5

1. Job 1:1
2. Job 2:3
3. Job 1:5
4. Job 1:16
5. Job 1:18, 19
6. Job 2:7
7. Job 30:27 and 30 NEB
8. Job 30:17, 18 NEB
9. Job 2:9
10. Job 30:19 NEB
11. Job 19:21
12. Job 4:7 NEB
13. Job 8:2 NEB
14. Job 11:2–6 NEB
15. Job 22:4–5 NEB
16. Job 22:21 and 30 NEB
17. Job 33:8–13 NEB
18. Job 34:10–12 NEB
19. Job 37:23, 24 NEB
20. Job 40: 3–5 NEB
21. Job 42:3–6 NEB
22. Job 1:9–11 NEB
23. Job 2:4–5 NEB
24. Job 2:10 NEB
25. Job 23:10
26. 1 Tim. 4:8

Chapter 6

1. John 15:13
2. John 10:18
3. John 19:11
4. 2 Cor. 5:19
5. John 3:16 AV
6. Matt. 27:46
7. Rom. 8:32
8. 1 John 4:10
9. John 3:16 NEB
10. John 20:21
11. Luke 9:23
12. Col. 1:24 NEB
13. 1 Pet. 2:21
14. Luke 14:27
15. Rom. 8:17

PART II

Chapter 1

1. Ex. 20:21 AV
2. Psa. 34:18
3. John 20:25
4. 2 Tim. 1:12 AV
5. Luke 23:46
6. Psa. 32:3, 4
7. Psa. 32:5
8. Isa. 6:3
9. Psa. 23:4
10. Heb. 11:6

Chapter 2

1. Rom. 8:28
2. Gen. 45:5 & 8
3. Gal. 1:15
4. Rom. 5:3–5

5. Rom. 8:37
6. Jude 21
7. Eph. 3:18–19
8. John 21:17

Chapter 3

1. 1 Cor. 3:21–23
2. Ex. 10:26
3. Heb. 2:15
4. John 6:67, 68

5. John 6:37
6. Isa. 43:1–3
7. Isa. 41:13

Chapter 4

1. John 12:24
2. John 12:27 & 28

3. Ex. 3:13

Chapter 5

1. John 6:37

2. 2 Cor. 12:7–10

Chapter 6

1. Heb. 11:3
2. John 18:11
3. 1 Cor. 2:9–10

4. 1 Cor. 1:21
5. Matt. 11:25, 26
6. Job 23:10